TRAVELS IN THE OTHER PLACE

PALLAVI AIYAR

TRAVELS IN THE OTHER PLACE

PURSUING THE SELF IN EIGHT ACTS

Published by Tranquebar, an imprint of Westland Books, a division of Nasadiya Technologies Private Limited, in 2025

No. 269/2B, First Floor, 'Irai Arul', Vimalraj Street, Nethaji Nagar, Alapakkam Main Road, Maduravoyal, Chennai 600095

ISBN: 9789371974950

10 9 8 7 6 5 4 3 2 1

Typeset by Jojy Philip

Printed at Parksons Graphics Pvt. Ltd

For
Julio

CONTENTS

BEGINNING

Do not tell me what you have studied, tell me how much you have travelled.

Anonymous

For a quarter of a century, I've been in geographic flux, making nests in eight countries across three continents. As a child I rarely left Delhi save on the pages of a book. Yet I grew up into a perpetual peripatetic—on the move as a reporter, tourist, wife, patient. And along the way I learnt something of the art of travelling well.

Travel can be a misleading term. In our everyday lexicon it refers to movement that privileges *space*, in the sense of going from one place to another. But travel is also woven into the texture of *time*. 'No man ever steps into the same river twice, for it is not the same river and he is not the same man,' said Heraclitus, the Greek philosopher. And indeed, we are not the same at eight as at eighteen or eighty. Life is a collage of temporal journeys through schools and marriages, hospitals and haircuts. Learning to travel well as an expat in a new country is practice, in many ways, for learning how to journey well through these vital chapters of being.

This book is inspired, in part, by the sixteenth-century French essayist Montaigne, in particular, the manner in which he transformed the individual quotidian into the collectively insightful. It takes the form of a series of travelogues knitted around universal milestones—from crossing over into what Susan Sontag called the 'kingdom of the sick', to learning to navigate the frontiers of Gen Z. The conclusion that links them all is that ultimately, every destination is enjoyable if appreciated for what it is, rather than disparaged for what it is not.

In China, where I lived in the early 2000s, the expat chorus groaned about malodorous toilets, natives spitting on the street, shoddy infrastructure, and 'inscrutable' locals. Personally, I found the services to be remarkably efficient—furniture made to order delivered in weeks, faulty plumbing fixed in hours. The food was a constant delight. The locals, once I learned Mandarin, were frank and funny. And the country was convulsing with epochal change, history unfolding in real time. Given this, disposing of toilet paper in a bin instead of flushing it was only onerous for those unable or unwilling, to see the rest of the panorama.

When I moved from Beijing to Brussels, European friends rejoiced for me. 'It'll be so much easier back home,' they said, oblivious to the fact that I did not share their 'home' either cartographically or imaginatively. 'Everything works there,' people sighed, misty-eyed at memories of flushing toilets. Europeans queue, I was assured. They don't spit.

But within half an hour of arriving, my bag was stolen—inside the Brussels airport—and I spent the next three years chasing unavailable plumbers. This was one way of looking at life in the city. And many of the expat crowd appeared determined to behold it in exactly this miserable manner. Brussels, they groaned, was a dirty place. No one cleaned up after their dog on the poo-punctuated streets. There was graffiti on the walls, and the city was rife with thieving immigrants from North Africa. Belgians were corrupt, lazy and unfriendly.

I grew to love Brussels: its coffee- and waffles-scented squares and the quirky art-nouveau architecture that unexpectedly popped up at the turn of a corner. I made local friends who floored me with their generosity. And the city was home to more chocolate shops than churches—just the right ratio.

Beijing and Brussels are as different as Sun Tzu and Jean-Claude Van Damme. But bad travellers complained about them in strangely similar ways. To paraphrase Tolstoy: all unhappy travellers are alike; every happy traveller finds their own path.

Travel in both its literal and symbolic avatars is the process of acquiring cognitive empathy. When you visit somewhere with different norms to those that you have known so far, the realisation dawns that those norms are not 'normal.' Every person's experience of the world is particular, but this specificity only becomes obvious when another way of being is accessed as a point of contrast. The greater the variety of lenses we acquire, the more skilled we become at embracing a range of perspectives, be these the norms of Japan or Mandarin or Cancer or Loss. At root, travelling well is about continuously expanding your identity by making the 'other' your own. It is to shape a luminescent shell whorl around your core, each layer adding texture, rather than erasing it.

And what a good traveller needs, above all, is attention. The ability not just to look, but see—with the kind of focus that allows meaningful details to emerge from undifferentiated experience. Lacking words can help. When you don't yet know the local language of a place, you walk around with all synapses firing—and really see how people hold themselves and how they laugh. Without language, you are displaced to the margins. And from the periphery you watch, filling in the gaps with little epiphanies. Acquiring a new language isn't only about grammar, but awareness—of vulnerability, of the invisible privilege of having *the right words*. Just as the real value of travelling to a new country is not a selfie in front of a monument, but what you learn about yourself, having gained an outsider's lens to train inward.

Finally, travelling well is a practice in gratitude for the journey, sharpened by the knowledge that it is finite. During the years I lived in Japan, watching cherry blossoms blaze in their brief beauty was a spring-time ritual. The feeling that sakura evoke is called mono no aware, a phrase that refers to the pain of the transience of things, laced with the knowledge that it is their very evanescence that makes them so beautiful.

There is one thing that you must do before you can travel-begin. As Montaigne, echoing Heraclitus, put it: 'Dare to be wise, begin: he who defers the hour of living well, is like the clown, waiting till the river shall have flowed out, but the river still runs on, and will run on, with constant course, to ages without end.'[1]

And so, let us begin.

1

BOOKS

There are metaphors more real than the people who walk in the street. There are images tucked away in books that live more vividly than many men and women …

Fernando Pessoa, *The Book of Disquiet.*

It's 1983. I am eight and prickling with excitement. In a few minutes, I will be sneaking out of my home's back door, tiptoeing to minimise the creaks. I will make my way down to the far end of the garden, where I will crouch, waiting for the signal. An owl-like hooting will mean that my friends are ready and around the corner. It's a moonlit night, so we will need to keep to the bogeyman shadows cast by the branches of the neighbourhood trees as we scuttle along.

Midnight picnics are magical. Something about sitting under the stars makes the potted tongue sandwiches extra delicious. And one of us can usually sneak out a bottle of sweet lemonade to wash it all down with. Mother and father have never got wind of these secret pleasures, although Timmy, our dog, has threatened to give it away on occasion. Tonight isn't just going to be about having a jolly time, although it always is when the five of us gather. We're also going to put on our thinking caps to figure out what to do about the hidden passageway. It's terribly narrow. And we'll need to enter sideways in single file. The opening is barely visible, a crack along the side of one of the smaller monuments on the edge of the tomb complex.

A few days ago, we'd been hunting down parakeet feathers in the gardens when Timmy had begun to bark uncontrollably. And then suddenly, we couldn't hear him any more except for a distant whine. We chased his cry, and that's how we stumbled upon the opening and the curious carvings along the walls of the passageway. We were going to try and follow it all the way down tonight. There was something not quite right about it. It smelled like … like ... dammit, all I could smell in that moment were alu ka parathas. Lunch was imminent, and my daydream came to a crashing halt.

It wasn't midnight, but noon. I had never seen, let alone eaten, a potted tongue sandwich. Our house did not have a back garden. No friends had ever hooted at me. I'd never been up after 9 p.m. And I'd never discovered a secret passageway.

I did have a dog called Timmy, but I wasn't allowed to take him out for walks by myself. He'd pounced on a passing dog once, and my uncle, who'd been holding him by a leash, had nearly toppled over. In fact, I wasn't allowed to leave the house on my own, period. An adult was always in tow, whether to the school bus stop or the local market.

I did occasionally hunt for parakeet feathers in the grounds of Humayun's Tomb. My family went for walks there on the odd weekend. The tombs had been built for the Mughal emperor Humayun, by his son, the emperor Akbar, 400 years before I ever stepped foot in them. But the neighbourhood in Delhi that I lived in, Nizamuddin, was nestled in the shade of these crumbling monuments. For adults, the backdrop had become mundane, opaque. But for children who hadn't yet forgotten to really look at the world, the tombs were alive with possibilities.

Much of Delhi was like that—ugly and traffic-clogged, but also punctuated with the carcasses of magnificent medieval buildings that offered alcoves and latticed windows and monsoon-swept terraces and bat-crowded crevices. Things to look through and climb under. Shapes and stones that fed the imagination. An imagination already fattened on Enid Blyton's *Famous Five* series.

In the early 1980s, India was liminal. We were like Schrodinger's cat, existing in two contradictory but equally true states. My generation of urban, upper-middle class Indians was post-colonial, having been born three decades after the British had vacated the country. But our tongues remained colonised by English, and a good part of our imagination too. The principal conquistador of the imagination wasn't a rapacious asset-stripper like Robert Clive or a quintessential aristocrat like Louis Mountbatten, but the daughter of a cutlery salesman from East Dulwich in London, who had never stepped foot in India: Enid Blyton.

It was through Blyton's *Faraway Tree* books of adventuring children that I, and many English-educated young people of my generation, first travelled elsewhere. We went to places where the summer was 'delightful' rather than the hellish onslaught of heat we knew it to be. We visited worlds where lacrosse-playing schoolgirls forgave errant foreigners for their transgressions, aware that they lacked an English sense of honour. We 'ate' scones and crumpets and quaffed ginger ale, exotic foods that seemed to be the essential accoutrement of Adventure.

Blyton's books never explained exactly what lacrosse, crumpets, or cornflowers were. The result was that, although they found a place in the ontologies of her Indian readers, they did so in purely imagined form. In those information-circumscribed days, one couldn't Google, so one fabricated. I imagined lacrosse to be a balletic exercise with butterfly-catching style nets, the ultimate goal of which remained hazy. Sardines, I envisaged as some kind of kebab. At eight, which for me was a *St Clare* school series–addicted age, I was even convinced that an English sense of honour was a 'thing.' And I wanted one.

I suffered from what Katherine Rundell calls the 'book worm's curse,'[1]: the problem of knowing the meaning of words without their pronunciation, never having heard them out loud. 'Pseudonym' gave me pause. And names like Penelope sounded like a combination of 'pen' and 'elope', until someone sniggered and corrected my pronunciation. Rundell recalls how she'd learned the word 'soporific' from Peter Rabbit and had been convinced that it had something to do with lettuces. I remember thinking 'putative' had some kind of rancid, disconcerting connotation. Somewhere I'd got it crossed with putrid.

The very act of reading as a child was like being set supervision-free in an adult world; a place where you had to rely on your wits to make sense of the experience. Mysterious words lurked in every other sentence. And it was only through the exploration of what lay on either side of them that meaning could be pieced together, bit by bit. Context, as all travel teaches, is key.

So many of the great writers of children's literature in English—Lewis Carroll, C. S. Lewis, E. Nesbit and Blyton—created worlds where parents were dead or gone. In their stories, children were always being abandoned, sent off to absent-minded uncles on remote islands, or packed off to school. But this was almost benign parenting in comparison to the nastiness of the fathers and stepmothers of fairy tales. Think Hansel and Gretel, where the children are forsaken in a forest by their own father. Or Cinderella, where evil family members force a little girl into servitude. Through books, the child reader is released from the strictures of their adult-determined lives and plunged into somewhere both terrifying and exhilarating, physically safe but emotionally dangerous.

With childhood travels through books on the mind, I asked my social media hivemind a question: 'Why did we all read so much Enid Blyton when we were kids? What was the attraction?' The thread blew up. Many said it was because we had few options. One friend answered, 'Er, colonialism?' There is probably some truth in both explanations.

We were Indian in lived experience, but having had our tongues English-ified, we read in English. And at the time, what bookshops offered in terms of English-language children's literature, was Enid Blyton. We didn't have easy access to stories translated from Indian languages. The only Indian stories I read were shoddily produced comic books of mythological tales from the Ramayana and Mahabharata. These were even more removed from our urban realities than Dorset—he setting for many of Blyton's adventure stories.

But several of the responses I received to my query also pointed to how, despite the seeming disconnect between the childhoods of Blyton's characters and our own, we found a way to build bridges from whichever Indian city we happened to be curled up reading in, to the southwest coast of England. We made that journey day after day, without moving from our bedrooms. We travelled, like humans did, on the pages of books.

One friend wrote, 'I remember those days when we had very little TV till the late 1980s. I remember being able to relate to tales from EB (Enid Blyton). I remember wanting to be similar—to be empowered to have adventure and fun'. I grew up in a small town, which was an overgrown village, where one could drink water from tube wells, fish in ponds, swim in rivers, climb trees, play with birds and butterflies. We were very much empowered to walk barefoot all over the town/overgrown village and then get back to EB. The exact feelings and memories cannot be expressed or explained. Pure innocence and joy.'

Another said, 'It was a magical world that I did not have access to in my physical or economic lived reality at that time, but it appealed to my formative sensibilities about where I would love to be. It was a world away from the world—so distant in reality, but so present in mine ... My neighbourhood friends and I, in sleepy Mysore, made our own versions of that life—

packed cucumber sandwiches and nimbu paani (homemade lemonade) and took off on our bicycles for a "picnic".'

And another: 'I think what appealed most was the way food was described in those books! From picnic lunches to treats in 'magic faraway lands.' But by the time I actually started travelling to the UK, most of it had been replaced by tikka masala.'

I have two boys. My older son was born in Beijing in 2008, the younger one in Brussels three years later. They went to kindergarten in Indonesia and primary school in Tokyo. As they became literate, I couldn't wait to introduce them to Enid Blyton's worlds. Watching them read and wander in their heads, I believed, would return me to being eight again; to the bated-breathness of chasing mysteries.

My fantasies around motherhood had always involved bedtime snuggles and books. The littles and I would sit together-apart, sharing our physical space but traveling with our own books, pausing only to sip contentedly from cups of chamomile tea. I wondered how their tastes might differ from mine. Who would be their most beloved character among the Famous Five? Would the *Mallory Tower* series have them begging to be sent off to boarding school as it had me?

In reality, neither of my boys made any headway with Blyton. They found the writing stilted, the idea of potted tongue gross. My younger one detests sardines. Lemonade and ginger ale—words I used to hold in my mouth with a shiver of anticipation for a world full of the exciting unexplored—held no power over them.

They preferred the tropical eastern islands of Indonesia to the windswept English coast, having experienced both firsthand. And they were flooded with a choice of reading materials, in addition to the Screen. They were so cosmopolitan and knowledgeable, travelled and bathed in abundance, that I realised I was foolish to think Blyton's tales would be their chosen repast. She had been food for the recently decolonised, pre-liberalisation mind. For my cyborgish children, her books were offal—sustenance for the deprived.

In my childhood, holidays and planes and hotels were rare. Doordarshan, the one state-owned television channel, went live for only a few hours in the evening, and its target audience was farmers pondering seed technology, rather than a young girl with magic on the mind. And so, reading was my most sustained experience of travel. Books had stood in for friends. Sometimes they'd stand in for dinner; I used to forget to feel hungry when I was in the grip of a good yarn.

My rational mind understands that it is futile to compare my proclivities as a child to those of my children, for they are creatures of a different paradigm. They have rarely known boredom, a prerequisite for learning how to read for pleasure. They've had lives so filled with gadgets and classes and play dates and physical travel that the space left over for books is meagre. Focus for their generation is a hyperlinked thing, which makes the linear, immutable book-ness of a book and the demands it makes on the concentration challenging.

We've had some arguments, my boys and I, about what they consider to be my exaggerated reverence for the Book. Reading is 'old fashioned,' I have been told. YouTube explainers are more efficient than non-fiction. TV series, documentaries and movies are better entertainment.

Yes, I splutter internally, but do you realise what is lost? What is lost is the stillness of mind that travelling through books brings to the reader; the very opposite of physical travel, which provokes a mental restlessness—a fear of missing out. Physical travel is often about a need for external validation—enter the selfie—that your trip is every kind of envy-generating superlative. Book travel is the most immersive kind, given that our minds are forced to engage with the writer's words to bring them alive. While reading, it is nigh impossible to dwell on the demonically dull to-do lists that form the architecture of our non-travelling every day. And a further advantage to journeying by book is that the traveller is unmolested by bad weather, logistics, lost credit cards or bad-tempered companions.

The writer and critic G. K. Chesterton, had counterintuitively argued that 'travel narrows the mind.' There was something tragic, he wrote in 1922, about the 'thoughtless tourist, who might have stayed at home loving Laplanders, embracing Chinamen, and clasping Patagonians to his heart in Hampstead or Surbiton, but for his blind and suicidal impulse to go and see what they looked like … The human bond that he feels at home is not an illusion. On the contrary, it is rather an inner reality. Man is inside all men … But to travel is to leave the inside and draw dangerously near the outside.'[2]

A hundred years on, I am surprised to find that I am beginning to agree, albeit with a smorgasbord of caveats, with curmudgeonly Chesterton. It is the first month of 2024. I am writing this first chapter of this memoir-as-travelogue in a remote corner of southwest Spain, with naught but a few books, olive groves and sheep for company. I rarely leave the house. After a quarter of a century of what can only be described as a frantically itinerant life, increasingly it is the standing-still variety of travel that appeals.

I begin reading a translation of the Portuguese writer Fernando Pessoa's aphoristic *The Book of Disquiet*. 'If I imagine, I see,' he writes. 'Only extreme poverty of the imagination justifies having to travel to feel.' Pessoa said that he knew only one 'real traveler with soul': an office boy who obsessively collected brochures, tore maps out of newspapers and memorised train schedules between far-flung destinations. The boy could recount sailing routes around the world, but he had never left Lisbon.

This put me in mind of a short story by the Indian-German writer Anita Desai, one I'd read in middle school, called 'The Sale'. I only remember the bare outline now, but it had made a powerful impression despite being perhaps the least critically feted of the *Games at Twilight* collection that it was part of. The story was very short and centred on a talented, but struggling, artist and his frenzied attempts to sell a painting—any painting—to politely disinterested visitors who happened to be browsing about his shambolic studio. The visitors are classic poverty porn–tourists, so titillated by the deprivation they are ogling that they fail to appreciate the virtuosity of the paintings. There are canvases filled with stunningly detailed flowers and assorted vital landscapes. But the twist in the tale lies in a throwaway remark towards the end of the story when the reader realises that the artist has never travelled away from his poor Bombay neighbourhood. His canvases have been painted entirely from the imagination.

I read Alain de Botton's *The Art of Travel*. He writes how easy it is to forget our restless, hungry, flatulent bodies when we contemplate travel and look at photographs of beautiful destinations. We imagine feeling perfectly and continuously happy as we project ourselves into the anticipated place. But, as he puts it, the body and mind are 'temperamental accomplices in the mission of appreciating (any) destination. The body found it hard to sleep, it complained of heat and flies and difficulties in digesting hotel meals … the mind meanwhile revealed a commitment to anxiety, boredom, free-floating sadness and financial alarm.'

There is an unsullied purity in the anticipated (and remembered) version of a place that is rarely experienced when one is corporeally there. And so, it is travelling through books that offers the purest form of peripatetic pleasure, by omitting and compressing the long periods of boredom and banality that accompany every physical trip. Book travel directs our attention to critical moments, which lend the travel a vividness and coherence it lacks in the actual execution.

I find a short essay written by my older son when he was seven years old. We had just returned to our home in Jakarta from a vacation to the island of Bali.

It reads:

Bali Holiday

> The first day in Bali, I went to a very nice restaurant and I ate without chewing. When we went to Bed I vomit and then I vomited again. But the next day I diden't. When it was the next day the whole family went swimming.

It is 2019. I am forty-four years old and reading aloud determinedly, in a small room in our apartment in Tokyo. My audience is my younger boy, now eight, who is running about making truck noises. I raise my voice slightly to be audible, if only to myself, over the din.

'Reading's just not my thing,' the boy had announced nonchalantly a few weeks ago. What did seem to be his 'thing' was watching endlessly inane YouTube videos of someone known by the nom de guerre Unspeakable, playing video games while chortling like a hyena at an Argentinian barbecue. When I recalled my own eight-year-old self, sneaking off in the imagination to the mysterious passageway in Humayun's Tomb, I was disappointed for my child. How much poorer he was, regardless of the material abundance he enjoyed.

Katherine Rundell's essay on why adults should read children's literature was a fixture by my bedside. 'It is to children's fiction that you turn,' she writes, 'if you want to feel awe and hunger and longing for justice: to make the old warhorse heart stamp again in its stall.' True enough. This old warhorse was champing at the bit. But my ponies had not got the memo.

I tried a regimen of enforced reading but could not make peace with the idea that, in doing this, I was training my child to equate reading with punishment. All of which had brought me to this moment, reading aloud to the eight-year-old, regardless of whether he appears to be listening or not.

In the months that follow, assisted by many cups of chamomile tea, I eventually wade through all three volumes of *The Lord of the Rings*, plus *The Hobbit*—that's about 1,500 pages—probably three-quarters of a year's worth of reading.

Blyton had already bombed with my older son, and so I'd thought to try Tolkien with the younger. What I had forgotten was just how great a part of these books involves interminable stretches of the characters walking. It is almost as if they are discursively mapping their inner selves through travel. After all, they are in the vein of epic mythological narratives, and travel and transformation are the primary tropes of these stories. In India´s great epics, the Ramayana and the Mahabharata, for example, the exiled heroes travel and quest, they wander and get lost, all to ultimately find themselves and their purpose. The same goes for the Buddha, Moses or the Daoist wayfarers.

As Gandalf says of Aragorn in *The Fellowship of the Ring*, 'Not all who wander are lost.' Rather, it is only those who wander that ultimately find.

When I was a teenager, Tolkein had spoken to me of the importance of fighting the good fight, of putting aside differences when needs must. A grand coalition of elves, dwarves, men, and eagles seemed to call for a pluralism that felt like a foundational value. But the books had not travelled across time as well as their protagonists traversed Middle-earth. As I read aloud night after night, intrusive, less-than-complementary thoughts pushed through constantly: Where are the women? Why are the elves so bloody blonde? Couldn't they hurry it up a bit while getting past Minas Morgul?

Travelling through a book, like travelling in the physical world, is as much about the reader/traveller's moment in life, what scars and lenses she brings to the experience, as it is about the book/destination.

Re-reading a book at two different points in one's life, like revisiting a place, is never the same experience? Your first time on a plane is exhilarating; your fiftieth, a trial to be endured with benzodiazepine assistance.

Of my childhood vacations in the mountains north of Delhi, I remember almost nothing but the sacred feeling their grandeur evoked. When I visit now, fresh from holidaying in the Swiss Alps, it's the plastic packaging strewn about the mountainsides that captures the attention. The more points of reference collected, the more relative the experience of travel inevitably becomes.

I might be getting on; jaded, though I fight it. But my boy is as fresh as an early spring day in Tokyo. We keep up the nightly readings. The only rule I insist on is that no screens are permitted while I read. He can choose to listen and be lulled into a world of magic rings and glamorous elves (male/white—I think quietly), or he can tune out and think his own thoughts about Unspeakable playing video games.

There are evenings when my son closes off his ears with his palms to drown out my words: I keep going, doggedly. Sometimes it feels like I am Frodo trudging to Mount Doom. There are evenings when the boy pleads with me to stop: I keep at it. And there are evenings when he babbles loudly to block my voice. I read on.

But then, there are evenings when he listens, his eyes growing large as he imagines Gandalf being rescued by the King of the Eagles, or an army of enraged tree-like Ents stomping towards the fortress of Isengard. I catch him with his mouth momentarily open, as though drinking in the images. He turns still despite himself; his opposition melting.

It took me almost two months of nightly reading before I heard the words that I had been thirsting for: 'One more page please, Mama.'

Slowly, softly, with shyness almost, my youngest began to approach books of his own accord. At thirteen, he now reads voraciously. He still watches an ungodly amount of YouTube, although fortunately, he discarded his proclivity for Unspeakable a few years ago. But he also reads. What got him truly immersed in *The Lord of the Rings* in the end were the maps. He would pore over them, putting cartographical detail into the travels of the Fellowship we read about. He had discovered the book as travel.

2

ILLNESS

Considering how common illness is, how tremendous the spiritual change that it brings, how astonishing when the lights of health go down, the undiscovered countries that are then disclosed, what wastes and deserts of the soul a slight attack of influenza brings to light, what precipices and lawns sprinkled with bright flowers a little rise of temperature reveals, what ancient and obdurate oaks are uprooted in us in the act of sickness, how we go down into the pit of death and feel the waters of annihilation close above our heads, while the whole landscape of life lies remote and fair, like the shore seen from a ship far out at sea.

Virginia Woolf, *On Being Ill*

It is the last month of 2022. I am forty-seven years old and squeezing my eyes closed to stem the tears, a hot river of pain that will not cease. The nurse sighs and speaks again. She is frustrated by my lack of words. By my lack of response, save these tears. '*Que pasó*?' she asks again, 'What's wrong?' There is a part of me that wants to cackle maniacally at the absurdity of the question. But something subterranean has shut down. By closing my eyes, I am refusing this situation. I am refusing the politeness that has been drilled into my good-girl depths since childhood. I am refusing the queries of someone trying to help me.

I've been a good soldier so far. Done what I've been told I must, unpleasant though it has been. I joked with the anaesthesiologist even as he was about to send me under. And whenever the oncologist asked how I was, I'd say, 'Well,' even though we were both aware of the inanity of the exchange.

But in this moment, my will to do what is necessary to 'fight,' has been overridden by my body. It is a corporeal act of rebellion against the monstrous loss of agency it has suffered. Against the indecency of having to submit. It does not want to be here. It does not want this bicycle-pump like syringe bearing down upon the remains of what used to be a breast. To be inflated with saline, week after week. It declines the cancer. It bites its thumb at this treatment.

I think of fattened chickens. Of flat tyres. Of my Frankenstein chest. The tears, which will not stop, are my body grieving itself. I'm not sure I'll ever be able to open my eyes again. Not until it, all of it, disapparates: the cutting and vomiting, the nurse with her syringe, saying 'thank you,' when the IV is inserted into the arm. I want my other passport back.

I had read Susan Sontag's *Illness as Metaphor* as a pretentious teenager. I was probably puffing on a cigarette as I read, glowing with youth, oblivious and unmarked. 'Everyone who is born holds dual citizenship, in the kingdom of the well and in the kingdom of the sick,' Sontag wrote. 'Although we all prefer to use only the good passport, sooner or later each of us is obliged, at least for a spell, to identify ourselves as citizens of that other place.'

And so it came to pass. The switching of the passports. Travels in that other place.

I'd felt a lump in my left breast on a late July day, four months prior to the moment I lay crying on the bed in the nurse's station.

I'd been putting together a jigsaw puzzle, and as I reached across the table to pick up a piece, the inner part of my upper left arm brushed against a lumpy intruder in my chest. It is difficult to find the word to describe that instant. Ricochet, maybe? There was the echo of an infinite array of women who had all lived this moment, this touch, this gasp. There was recognition in the heartbeat when my fingers touched the skin, to find it unyielding, uncompliant. This world came undone. In a slow blink, I stepped into the other place, somewhere I no longer had plans, only hospital appointments. I had long advocated travel outside one's comfort zone in my writings. Now I would walk the talk.

I made an appointment to see my GP the next morning and, in the meantime, tried to quell the electric shock of discovery by not talking about it. It was my last day with my brother, who had been visiting us in Madrid for a long weekend. We went out for lunch to one of the elegant cafés around the Puerta de Alcalá gate.

There was a frisson of excitement as we discovered the bald man at the table next to ours was Zinedine Zidane, famous footballer and head-butter. We spent lunch agonising over whether or not to ask him for a selfie, not wanting to appear gauche, but also eager for the social media excitement a photo with him would generate. In the end, we swallowed our misgivings, sidled up to him and asked. Zidane looked bored, but nodded assent. At the exact moment the waiter, pressed into service to take the photograph, tapped on the camera button, he broke into a practised, 1,000-watt smile.

For the rest of the day, worries about my lump were submerged in the chatter, the photo-trophy and the chorus of, 'Oh, my God, can you believe that was Zidane?'. That evening, my brother departed for his home in the United States, and I went to bed in relative peace.

But when I woke the next morning, my breathing was ragged. Looking back, although Google had reassured me that the majority of lumps are not cancerous, my bones knew. I couldn't look the word in the eye at that point. Ever since the jigsaw-puzzle-arm-brush-lump moment the day before, CANCER had been lurking on the sidelines of my consciousness. But as soon as it tried to push its way onto centre stage, my sensible mind beat it back into the shadows.

The GP was poker-faced as he asked me to remove my bra. I didn't know then how that action—removing my bra—would be repeated so often that it would almost become second nature. I would enter a doctor's cabin and automatically begin disrobing in preparation, to offer up my breast, for squeezing, puncturing—whatever happened to be on the day's medical menu. In the ensuing weeks, I'd visit a smorgasbord of specialists, including an ophthalmologist who looked bewildered when I began to unbutton my shirt unbidden, until comprehension made her sad. 'No, you're here for your eyes,' she'd said gently.

The GP confirmed the lump. 'It's probably nothing,' he said, but advised me to get a mammogram and ultrasound as soon as possible, 'to rule out …' His words tailed off. The Word that could not be looked at directly remained in the shadows. It was August, the dog days of summer in Spain. The family and I were due for a week's holiday in the cooler climes of Galicia. All the bookings had been made months ago. Did I need to call the plan off, I asked? 'No, no,' the doctor replied, wiping beads of sweat off his forehead. Madrid was an oven. It would take a while to get test results back, and I'd needlessly torture myself by staying in the heat.

The next day, I was at a breast clinic, answering odd-seeming questions from the mammogram technician. Ones I would be asked again and again, like some kind of immigration test for a new country. The age that I got my period. The age that I had my first child. This one led to some unintended hilarity on account of my imperfect Spanish. I thought the technician was asking the age of my first child, rather than the age I gave birth to him. Thirteen, I replied, causing her a moment of consternation until we sorted out the crossed signals. How long did I breastfeed my first child for? And the second one? The questions continued.

I learned that getting your period before the age of twelve, having your first child after the age of thirty, and choosing not to breastfeed are all risk factors in developing breast cancer. Most breast tumours (in the event, mine as well) are hormone positive. What does this mean?

Breast cancer cells have receptors, a type of protein, that attach to oestrogen and progesterone—the chief pregnancy hormones. The longer a woman menstruates, the higher her lifetime exposure to these hormones and the greater the likelihood of hormonophile cancer cells developing to grab on to them. Conversely, pregnancy and breastfeeding, both of which reduce the number of a woman's periods over a lifetime and, as a result her cumulative vulnerability to ovarian hormones are associated with a decrease in breast cancer risk.[1]

In sum: the less time one spends being pregnant and breastfeeding in one's fertile years, the higher the likelihood of developing breast cancer. For women, it's biological sabotage; the cosmic curse of a patriarchal God. 'Go forth and procreate or else it's off with your breasts.'[2]

Who knew? I didn't. Or maybe I had read something, somewhere and had just filtered it out. There is only so much risk we can be alive to, in order to behave like we are living instead of dying—both of which happen to be true, of course.

During my travels in Cancer that would follow, I was often dogged by a sense of déjà vu. And it took me a while to figure out that the source of this resonance was my past journeying in Pregnancy. Even the word for breast cancer in Spanish, cáncer de mama, was maternal. Mama the person, and the breast that fed her motherhood into being, were indistinguishable in the language.

Breast cancer and pregnancy are landscapes bound together in their womanliness, their concerns with nipples and hormones, and the manner in which they involve an alien presence within the body of the host. In her essay, Sontag quotes the eighteenth-century German polymath, Novalis, defining cancers as, 'full-fledged parasites—they grow, are engendered, have their structure, secrete, eat.' And St Jerome, she adds, had this to say about the disease, 'The one there with his swollen belly is pregnant with his own death' (*Alius tumenti aqualiculo mortem parturit*).

The metaphor of cancer as foetus has pedigree, I thought. The next day, we left for our summer vacation in Galicia.

Pregnancy and Cancer share a climate: guilt. It is confounding how much blame, both subtle and direct, the pregnant and the cancerous are subject to, because of what they might have been eating. You ate too much sugar, you had a smoke, you didn't manage stress, you didn't exercise enough—or was it too much? No matter: it's your fault.

Reading about what could have 'caused' my cancer was laughably like the reading I'd done when pregnant: full of warnings of dangers lurking in the microwave.

A teratogen is a substance that is potentially harmful to a developing embryo or foetus. And these pesky things are everywhere. They live in hot tubs, ibuprofen, microwaves, cling foil, anti-perspirants and hair dye, among an Odyssey-long list of other innocent-looking stuff. And there is 'research' to show that all of these could also be carcinogenic.

Everyone had an opinion on what I should eat when I was pregnant: no cheese, no sushi, no cold foods—or was it hot ones? No matter: my diet had been every well-intentioned person's business. Once my body turned tumorous, this public jurisdiction over what I ingested staged a comeback. When people—some whom I knew well, others whom I'd just met—learned of my diagnosis, many took it upon themselves to send me lists of alkaline foods and cancer-starving ones; no-sugar diets and all manner of juices I could apparently take to replace chemotherapy.

New lands have their own cultural conventions. And in both Pregnancy and Cancer, there is an age-old belief that a woman's attitude—and the degree of its positivity—influences the outcome: a smooth pregnancy, a calm baby, remission from cancer. The implicit implication of this hoary tradition is that if someone has a difficult pregnancy, a colicky baby, or breast cancer metastasis, it is her fault for having failed to radiate positivity, even as her body is split wide open. She has failed to believe in the goodness of her suffering.

I already knew, from my pregnancies, the process by which one becomes a stranger to oneself. How the dressing-table mirror takes on the avatar of its reflection-distorting funfair cousins. It is you who looks in, but something other that looks back out.

The kingdom of Cancer is a terrain of high mountains, deep troughs, and even some wildflower-carpeted valleys. The tallest mountain here is called the Diagnosis. It takes time, stamina and second opinions to climb this one. And often, just when you think you're cresting the summit, you realise the actual peak has been shrouded in mist.

I was sipping my coffee, off the white-sand beach of Galicia's Cíes Islands, gulls circling and children running happily amok, when the mobile phone rang. It was the clinic. Bad news. Bottom line: I needed to come in as soon as possible for a biopsy. They emailed me the results, which I read on my phone, while the boys built a sandcastle less than ten feet away. The document said something about BI-RADS 5.

I felt plunged underwater, my ears filled with a roaring, my lungs starved of oxygen. I began to Google this cipher of letters and numbers slowly, as though having to move through something viscous. It was my first step in learning the new language of this kingdom, Oncolish. BI-RADS stood for 'Breast Imaging and Data System,' a standardised system to describe mammogram findings and results. The number 5 indicated the highest possible suspicion of malignancy—over 95 per cent.

It would be two days before we could return to Madrid for the biopsy. The dichotomy between my outside calm with the children and the inferno of fear that raged inside me was surreal. Externally, I marvelled at the diversity of seabirds. Internally, all thoughts led to death. The word that could not be looked at directly was now yanking my head up by the hair to force me to meet its eye. It was a cursed word, CANCER, heavy with baldness and coffins. It was the end of happiness. The monstrous crab under the bed.

I imagined my funeral. There was some pleasure in this. Fantasising about other people's potential eulogies was flattering. 'She was such a kind person ... sensitive writer ... good friend ... great fun.' But then I would think of my boys, of their bereavement, and was instantly undone.

Back in Madrid, I went in for the biopsy on the very afternoon of our return. I was as terrified about the process itself as the results. A needle was inserted into my breast a few times to gather samples from the 'suspicious' mass, the squatter in the mammary. It occurred to me, even as my chest was being punctured, what a writerly quality there is to this disease. Sontag had riffed on how cancer wasn't an illness of time, as much as 'a pathology of space.' So much about it was topographic—spread and proliferation.

My breast wasn't the only body part to be biopsied. A lymph node in my armpit had appeared inflamed on the ultrasound and also needed to be checked out. When breast cancer spreads, it does so first to the lymph nodes under the arm, closest to the affected breast. If these are found to be cancer-free, it means the malignant cells have yet to make a jailbreak from their point of origin.

Two days later, I had the results of the biopsies—much to the shock of my friends in the UK who, throughout this process, appeared more interested in the speed with which the medical juggernaut in Spain preceded than with the fact of my cancer itself. I forgave them. They had their own cross to bear with the NHS post-Brexit.

We met with a doctor at the clinic to discuss the findings. He smiled when we walked in and the knots in my stomach instantly relaxed. *Oncolish*, like all languages, is as much about learning to read body language as it is about the rules of grammar. In Cancer, a doctor's smile is like winning the lottery. And this was exactly what it appeared I had done.

My tumour, the doctor explained, was in situ, in its place of origin. It hadn't begun wandering yet; it remained 'non-invasive.' It was at stage-0. And my lymph node biopsy was clear. I would need a lumpectomy—a surgery that would remove just the tumour, leaving most of the breast intact—and then perhaps a few sessions of radiation after. No chemo. 'You're a lucky woman,' he concluded.

My husband and I left the clinic flooded with relief. We drank vanilla milkshakes to celebrate. I wondered aloud if I could put off the surgery for a few months, until I was done teaching a semester at the prestigious university that had recently offered me a job. We marvelled at modern medicine and our antiquated notions of the horror of cancer.

The next day, I decided to dive into an intensive course of the new idiom of the kingdom I was temporarily in. And so, I bought the promising-sounding, *The Complete Guide to Breast Cancer: How to Feel Empowered and Take Control*.

I learned that 'Non-invasive breast cancer (ductal carcinoma in situ or DCIS) develops in the cells of the breast ducts. This cancer does not have the ability to spread to other parts of your body.' But there was more. 'If DCIS is not treated,' I read on, 'it may develop into an invasive cancer in the months or years ahead.'

By the end of the day, the elation of my super-early-stage diagnosis began to wear thinner. Everything had moved so quickly, and as a seasoned traveller, I was suspicious of seemingly pothole-free paths. The clinic I'd been to was well regarded, but it would be prudent to get a second opinion. And for this, I headed to Madrid's largest private cancer hospital.

Four hundred employees, including oncologists of every kind, worked there. It reminded me of an airport terminal. The registration front desk, down to the uniforms of the staff, was reminiscent of flight check-ins. The nurses were like air hostesses, asking you to take a seat, and the doctors like pilots, telling you not to worry, it was just a bit of turbulence. The place was teeming. I was gobsmacked by the demographic diversity: so many people with cancer—high-society women and taciturn teenagers, the disoriented elderly, and tech bros who didn't stop taking calls even as they were being wheeled away.

My second-opinion oncologist looked at my biopsy results without comment, her face deadpan. Then, instead of congratulating me on the DCIS good news, she said that I needed more tests before she could proffer judgement. These included a triumvirate of scans: MRI, PET and CAT. I had to learn more Oncolish as I was injected with radioactive dyes and placed in various machines. But on the whole, I felt as though I was taking control, just as the book I'd bought advised. It was good to have lots of extra information, I thought, despite the hassle and delay and needles and having to stay still in jackhammering metal coffins for what felt like geological epochs.

It took a few days for all the scan results to be ready (British friends continued to be stunned by the speed of the process).

My second time back at the second-opinion oncologist's cabin had her looking even glummer than round one. The good news, she said, looking about as joyous as a teenage boy facing an empty fridge, was that there did not appear to be any metastasis of my tumour. I immediately tensed in anticipation of what she'd say next. The bad news.

It transpired that the doctor did not 'like' the images that had shown up on my MRI. These were not in 'concordance' with a diagnosis of DCIS. The tumour looked more threatening than an innocent in situ; it had the countenance of an invader. Another biopsy was needed, a vacuum-assisted one, which was capable of garnering more detailed pathological information than the simple needle biopsy I had already had.

A vacuum-assisted biopsy or VAB, uses a special instrument to suck up a larger amount of cellular material than a needle can. It's like running a high-quality, ultrasound-guided, vacuum cleaner inside your breast, gathering up detritus, dust motes, scuttling crabs.

Getting the VAB was my first experience of my body in revolt. A precursor to the breast-inflating rejection to come a few months later. After all the emotions of the preceding weeks: finding lump, having mammogram, getting results on beach, biopsy 1 good news, second opinion, horrid tests, potentially less good news—the constant need to recalibrate had my mammaries feeling ornery, reluctant to submit. But the right of refusal did not form part of the constitution of this kingdom. It truly was a shitty passport, even worse than the Indian one, which required visas to travel virtually anywhere. With this passport, all travel was a staycation.

Another week, another set of results, another meeting with the oncologist. The cancer cells, as the new biopsy confirmed, had begun to travel. They were no longer *in situ* in the ducts—the tubes that carried maternal milk to the nipple—but had begun drifting into the rest of the breast. I had invasive breast cancer. This was stage 1. Diagnosis was a steeper mountain than I had thought it would be. The climb had me quite out of breath.

A lumpectomy was scheduled, despite my surgeon having made some noises about my small breasts and less-than aesthetic outcomes. Lumpectomy was the psychologically and physically kinder, new standard *operating* procedure for breast cancer, having replaced the radical mastectomy that was *de rigueur* a generation ago.[3] I would also have what is called a sentinel node biopsy, another breast cancer SOP.

Sentinel node is possibly my favourite term in *Oncolish*, being unusually metaphorical for a tongue so densely populated with acronyms and numbers. It refers to the lymph node that the breast directly drains into, the first line of the body's defence—the sentinels that raise the alarm. If the sentinels are clear, the crab is contained. If they are breached, the enemy is likely aboard.

The day before my surgery, my younger son came to find me. He handed me a note I'd scribbled that he'd come across on my desk. 'Have you been writing a poem about your cancer?' he asked. This is what I'd written:

> Lumpectomy or mastectomy.
> Exercise for my arm.
> When can I start walking?
> Guests at the hospital.
> And how much will it hurt?
> The chemo—how bad?
> Anaesthesia, need anti-nausea meds.
> Can I elevate my arm—Or not?

With this found poem, and the pride I felt in my offspring's eyes that saw the poetry, I was able to face the prospect of the approaching knife with a measure of calm.

I was home from the lumpectomy—an overnight stay in hospital later. The tumour had been excised. My breast looked like a Rottweiler had taken a bite out of it, but it was still very much there. And I felt perky. I went out for a short walk a day later, and by the time of my next hospital appointment, I was positively bouncy.

But the moment I entered the doctor's office and registered her pinched face, the bounce left me. The pathology results were back.

The tumour margins were not clear—Oncolish for some cancer cells were detected beyond the area that had been cut out. I would need more surgery to clear these.

My sentinel node, 'surprisingly,' the doctor said, was infected.

Moreover, the infected node displayed extracapsular extension, which meant the cancer cells were threatening to extend outside the lymph node capsule—they were poised to breach.

This was a triumvirate of 'adverse pathological features'. My cancer was now staged at 2-B, a product of the size of my tumour and lymph node involvement. I had finally crested the summit of Diagnosis, and it had been a gruelling climb.

I realised in that moment that my oncologist had never asked me much about myself, or at least what I had understood to be the 'self,' pre-cancer. I had imagined this to be some inner essence comprising my likes and aversions, my achievements, my psychological traumas. But for the doctor, my 'self' was mostly biomechanics. We discussed white blood cell counts and kidney function. She didn't ask what college I'd been to, what awards I'd won, what books I'd written. All those markers of what I'd supposed amounted to 'success' were superseded by my faulty cells. My body was 'Made in India'. German engineering boasted the longevity of its wares, but in India, we were creatures of jugaad and air pollution.

It was decided, in consultation with my surgeon, that I would have a full mastectomy and axillary node dissection, followed by five months of chemotherapy using two different drug regimens, topped off with five years of hormone-suppressing tablets. If the remaining lymph nodes excavated during the dissection were clear, I could avoid radiation therapy. If not, I would also be irradiated daily for several weeks.

Systemic treatment, as chemo is referred to because it treats the whole body as a system rather than just a localised part, like a breast, is an insurance policy against recurrence. Once the crab is afoot, all bets are off. It can be sneaky and hide out of sight of scans for years.

A couple of hundred years ago, systemic remedies for cancer included tincture of lead, extracts of arsenic, boar's tooth, fox lungs, goat's dung, tortoise liver.[4] But since the mid-twentieth century, chemo is the best available armament in the medical arsenal to blow up the crafty crustacean before it has the chance to grab any more real estate.[5] This is, however, a bit like dropping a nuke to get a cockroach, and even an H-bomb is no guarantee against a roach.

The risks of all these interventions include cardiotoxicity, osteoporosis, arthritis, lymphoedema, and—wait for it—other cancers. A potential side effect of most cancer treatments is more cancer—called 'secondary cancers'. You have to laugh, because what else can you do?

Well, I suppose you could cry. Which is exactly what I did, and in such volumes that it was as if an internally contained glacier had melted. After weeks of having girded myself to 'fight' the battle—that is the cancer patient's clichéd duty—I was feeling defeated. I suppose being told I would have chemotherapy was what felled me. Having been conditioned by images of bald-headed emaciation, I dreaded this lower case 'c' more than the Big C itself.

Until the treatments began, I'd been quite well. I'd had energy, my skin glowed. My blood results were those of someone in the pink of health. The cancer had not manifested any symptoms—save the lump—and the mastectomy had taken care of that. The disease was an intellectual reality, but I didn't feel ill. It was the cure, the chemo, that would sicken me.

I remember precisely the moment I felt the desolation lift. I was sitting at the kitchen table, in the tears that had become my daily companions, when I grabbed a pen and began scribbling on a piece of paper. 'It's all plot,' I wrote. Instantly, my heart lightened. I would recast the horrors of Diagnosis as story, as travel, and learn to appreciate this place on its own terms, rather than to compare it unfavourably to what it was not. This, after all, was always my advice to new expats in a foreign country.

From the perspective of narrative, feeling unwell is more interesting than being well. And how marvellous that I happened to be a writer. That evening, I thumbed through my copy of Hillary Mantel's memoir, *Giving up the Ghost*. Mantel's life had been riddled by pain and illness from childhood. But it was also leavened by imagination and the ability to look at herself from a distance.

Through adolescence, she suffered from various misdiagnoses including hysteria and mental disease at the hands of a conspiracy by smug and incompetent male doctors, until she was able to self-diagnose her condition as endometriosis. This is an agonising condition wherein the tissue that is supposed to line the inside of the uterus—the endometrium—grows outside of the organ.

If left untreated, the womb lining then migrates to locations it has no business being in, such as on the ovaries or within the peritoneal cavity. It 'metasises'. By the time Mantel got treatment in 1980, at the age of twenty-seven, she was subjected to the removal of her womb, ovaries and part of her bowels and bladder. She woke up from the surgery to premature menopause and infertility. Later, years of ingesting hormone replacement tablets changed her body's contours—both the visible and invisible parts.

Writing was her way of surviving the ghosts of her unborn children and the pain that was her constant companion. 'I wrote and wrote,' she said. Even as she got sicker, she kept writing. 'Bald, odd-shaped, deaf but not defeated, I sat down and wrote another book.' Writing was the one activity she could do while being prone. 'I was seethingly ambitious ... I needed to be somebody,' Mantel spoke to me across the years and pages. 'The only way I could think of was by writing. Because all you need is paper and pencil, and you can do it horizontal.'

I rose from the kitchen table, refuelled. Words would prop me up. With a story, I could make it through, even if rendered horizontal.

The night before my mastectomy, I felt very aware of my breast, the feel of the nipple against the material of my nightshirt. How does one say farewell to a part of oneself? 'It's been a good breast,' I wrote in my diary, 'tingling pleasurably at the appropriate moments, and feeding the boys when they needed it.'

Cancer, as Sontag had pointed out, is irredeemably metaphorical, several common iterations of which I disliked. I did not like the image of 'fighting' cancer, because it was not a war. I did not feel like I was 'surviving' it either, at least no more than everyone alive is 'surviving' life, the only certainty of which is death. And I certainly did not desire to 'fuck,' it.

The metaphor that gave me succour was the thought of my breast as a Sakura—the Japanese word for cherry blossom. I'd lived in Tokyo for four years and every spring, the day of their blossoming had felt miraculous; the streets blushing shades of pink and the very air aglow. But what made the sakura profound was not their beauty as much as their brevity.

I had a tendency to suffer from anticipatory nostalgia. It was rare for me to experience something wonderful without that experience being tinged with the pathos of its imminent passing. The balletic swirl of steam rising from a cup of jasmine tea in a Chengdu teahouse would already have me missing that specific scent at some unspecified time in the future. Or I'd be sitting by the sea in eastern Indonesia, the horizon so huge I couldn't help but believe that a bit further and I'd fall off the edge of the earth. Yet mixed in with the magic, would be a prescient nostalgia for that irreplicable moment.

In Japan, I learned that this feeling had a name: mono no aware, a phrase that referred to the pain of the finiteness of things, laced with the knowledge that transience is an essential part of their beauty.

Haiku master Matsuo Bashō's (1644–1694) encapsulated the idea pithily when he wrote:

> Between our two lives
> there is also the life of
> the cherry blossom.

The future nostalgia of mono no aware enhances the experience of the now. It is the knowledge of the evanescence of this moment that you imagine missing later on, which allows you to submit fully to it.

The companion of serious illness is a loss of innocence; of the sense that life is stable and reliable, that our being is substantial, solid. And so, I felt for my bosom sadness at having to bid it goodbye, but also a heightened awareness that impermanence is a profound truth. Mine was not the world's most beautiful mammary, but on the surgeon's table, it would be gorgeous, in the very moment that it was being scooped out and discarded.

The surgery went well enough. And to my great relief, no further lymph nodes, among the dozen removed, were infected. I'd also simultaneously had what was billed as 'immediate' breast reconstruction.

The one corner of Cancer that felt most, 'when life gives you lemons, make lemonade,' was the principality of the Plastic Surgeon. It was the area where waiting patients heard chuckles emanating from within the closed doors of the consultation room. It's where the doctors looked like movie stars. It was the candy shop of cancer.

My first meeting with the plastic surgeon, began with something akin to banter. Unlike the oncologist, he wasn't solely preoccupied with my disease. He asked me about the kinds of books I wrote. He told me I had 'cute shoes.' As a matter of fact, I did. I had purchased the neon green footwear with patterned yellow butterflies while on vacation in Barcelona. But no one—MRI technician, oncologist, surgeon, radiologist, anaesthesiologist—had commented on these cuties before.

Plastic surgeons had an eye for the aesthetic. They were also all, in the hospital that I was visiting, male. The oncology department was ruled by queens. But the domain of cosmetic surgery was commandeered by three men. The gender division was so stark that I Googled it as I whiled away time at the hospital. I discovered that in the United States, only about 18 per cent of breast reconstructions are done by female surgeons.[6] Women's breasts, unsurprisingly, to anyone with an interest in the history of female bodies, are largely in the hands of men.

As my own appointment with the plastic surgeon progressed, I had to strip from the waist up and pose in various directions while the doctor took photos of my breasts. Boob-modelling session over, a discussion ensued involving enhancing the 'volume' of my bosom. When I demurred, insisting that I just wanted the one breast reconstructed to its original proportions, the doctor looked sorrowful. 'Are you sure, sure?' he inquired, and I felt the worm of insecurity wiggle into my brain. Was there something wrong with my 'volume'?

Sticking to my guns, I insisted that I was 'sure, sure.' The surgeon shrugged. 'You can always change your mind,' he said with an annoyingly knowing look, as if thinking, 'they always do,' and handed me a card with his personal number. 'Feel free to WhatsApp me anytime.'

Next, it was time for my un-mastectomied breast to be the centre of unaccustomed attention. The plan for this one, the doctor explained, would be to, 'put it back in its original place.' This euphemism for lifting my saggy old boob felt slightly insulting but given the probing and puncturing my body had suffered by this point, saggy boobs came in low in the hierarchy of affronts. Once again, I rejected the offer, and once again, the surgeon reiterated that I could change my mind further down the road. For it was going to be a long and winding route.

What had appealed to me most about the idea of a breast reconstruction was its label: 'immediate.' The propinquity of the phrasing had a mitigating effect on the horror of the imminent amputation. In fact, I soon learned that both 'immediate' and 'reconstruction' were misnomers. The process involved multiple surgeries and the end result was a mound of flesh sans nipple or sensation, slashed through with a wide scar. It bore about as much resemblance to a Pamela Andersonesque bikini chest, as Harrison Birtwistle does to Beethoven.

For women who are likely to have post-mastectomy chemo or radiotherapy, the only thing immediately inserted into the cavity left by a mastectomy is something called a tissue expander. This is an empty implant placed behind the pectoral muscle, directly after the removal of the breast. You must then visit the hospital every few weeks over the next several months to have the expander inflated with saline, delivered through an enormous syringe that is struck directly into the implant. In this way, the 'breast' is gradually pumped up into the desired shape. As the expanders fill, they stretch the tissue and cause new skin to grow, so that eventually there is enough to cover the final implant, which is swapped with the expander.

Immediate? Words that sound the same in the kingdom of the sick and that of the well are often false friends.

If Diagnosis was the highest mountain of Cancer, then Chemo was its lowest trough. I started infusions the day after my forty-seventh birthday, a month after the mastectomy.

A week earlier, I'd had a catheter threaded through the vein in my arm, all the way to somewhere next to my heart. It was almost incomprehensible that these things were being done to me. That I now had a tube crawling through my body like a tape worm, exposing my heart to the world.

In Oncolish, this tube is called a PICC (peripherally inserted central catheter) line. And it was going to live in my body for the next five months, the duration of the chemo regimen. All my infusions would be given through it. My blood draws would be taken from it. It eliminated the necessity for repeated poking for anyone due to be poked a lot.

I hated the PICC. Hated having to cover it with a plastic dressing before taking a shower. Hated having to visit the hospital every single week to have it tended to by a nurse. Hated the skin irritation around the site of insertion. Hated how vulnerable it made me feel—a yank away from rupture. It was a gaping hole straight into my body's inner sanctum. A twenty-four-hour–reminder of my patienthood.

Then I started chemo, and the PICC descended lower on the list of things I hated.

The standard chemo protocol for early-stage breast cancer is to treat the patient sequentially with two different types of chemotherapeutic agents. One type belongs to a class of drugs called anthracyclines, and the other to a group known as taxanes.[7] Alkylating agents are also mixed in, usually in combination with the anthracycline.

All these drugs kill rapidly dividing cells—speedy division being a characteristic of cancer cells. But they also affect healthy cells that just happen to naturally divide quickly, like those in the bone marrow, digestive tract, and hair follicles. Hence, the nausea, hair loss and immunosuppression that we are primed to associate with cancer.

How they differ is in their mechanisms of action, as well as in their side effects. Not all chemo is equal. The anthracycline-alkylating agent combo took me through the most hellish part of the kingdom of the sick. In contrast, the taxane treatment was but a fatigued walk in the park.

Chemo is given in cycles, with each infusion followed by a recovery period, to allow the non-cancerous healthy cells decimated by the drugs to limp back to some kind of normality in between sessions. I was started on a combination of the anthracycline epirubicin, combined with cisplatin, an alkylating agent. This cocktail, known by the acronym EC, was given to me every two weeks and repeated for a total of four cycles.

Epirubicin is an anti-tumour antibiotic that works by interfering with the enzymes involved in copying cellular DNA during the cell cycle. Enzymes are proteins that assist or speed up the rate of chemical reactions in cells. Anthracyclines like epirubicin render the cells they affect, sterile—unable to reproduce. Cisplatin does something similar. But as these two go about attacking cancer cells, EC, as they are known to their intimates, also decimate the white blood cells of the person receiving them. The nausea/vomiting dial is turned up high. Full hair loss also occurs, usually after the second dose. Menstruation stops. Darkness descends, and it feels like winter.

After EC, I was put on weekly infusions of Taxol, a kind of taxane, for twelve weeks. Taxanes are compounds derived from natural products, like plants. They work in some other jargon-filled way to disrupt cancer cells, but are notable for being lighter on the nausea and gentler to the white blood cells. Not that they are entirely benevolent either. Their preferred legacy is neuropathy of the hands and feet, a damaged liver and peeling off nails.

And fatigue is every chemo agent's companion. The kind of deep, in-your-bones, tiredness that makes even thinking about a time when you didn't feel tired, tiring.

I went into chemo with a wealth of knowledge of what to expect from those with first-hand experience of it. Since my diagnosis,

I'd been surprised to discover just how cancerous the world is. There was hardly a person with whom I shared my condition, who failed to tell me about an aunt, a mother, or best friend with the same disease. It's a pandemic, was a common refrain. Indeed, one in seven women in the European Union develop breast cancer at some point in their life.[8]

Being open about my tumour meant that I discovered how fragility binds humans into a community that is robust because of its collective vulnerability. Writing about illness lit up the nodes connecting me to fellow travellers in the kingdoms of the sick, the broken and the imperfect.

Vulnerability is a constellation of care made up of long-forgotten primary school classmates, the cousins of friends and the friends of cousins. We are all in various stages of being blindsided, sad or accepting of the decay of our mortal flesh—for if we are human, decay we will. And yet, how difficult it remains to accept this as fact.

In the early days of my treatment, I read *Figuring*, a book by essayist and literary curator Maria Popova. It was a complex read, at the intersection of poetry and science, biography, and philosophy. Amongst the brilliant cast of intellectually striving characters brought to life in its pages was Caroline Herschel, the world's first professional female astronomer, discoverer of eight comets and calculator of the locations of 2,510 nebulae. Herschel also suffered from pain for almost the entirety of her life, having barely survived typhus at the age of eleven, an affliction that left her half blind and stunted.

Popova quotes from a letter that an eighty-one-year-old Herschel wrote to her niece, 'My complaint is incurable, for it is a decay of nature … What a shocking idea it is to be decaying. *decaying*!'

Popova concludes, 'Our psychology (today) has remained just as vulnerable to the shock of our mortality, the emotional upheaval of which endures unpalliated by reason.'

Even while I was climbing Diagnosis, I had noticed a sorority forming around me. I got a call from a former university professor whom I hadn't been in touch with for about two decades. She had just finished breast cancer treatments a year earlier and wanted to let me know she was there if I needed her. The mother of one of my younger son's classmates dropped by with flowers. She'd had a double mastectomy four years ago. In Madrid, a friend who was five years out of treatment, drove me to the hospital on the occasions that my husband was unavailable. Another sent me a jigsaw puzzle and scented soaps in the mail from the UK, even as she was undergoing radiation herself.

The Japanese women I used to learn taiko drumming with in Tokyo, couriered an enormous box with my favourite convenience store snacks, photographs of our old performances together, and a Shinto prayer charm blessed by the abbot of a well-known temple. My taiko teacher's partner, an Australian woman, had been diagnosed with breast cancer barely six months before me. I hadn't known her in Tokyo, but on learning of my situation, she began writing almost weekly. We became cancer pen pals.

Chemo had been very arduous for some who'd undergone it and indifferent for others. Each body experiences the drugs differently. Most said they had forgotten what it really felt like, in the way the female body tends to develop amnesia about the pain of childbirth. Some advised me to ice my feet while getting the infusions to help prevent neuropathy. Others said to take an extra blanket. Everyone recommended rest. However bad you might feel at any one moment, they reminded me, you will not feel like that always.

And so I arrived for my first infusion at the hospital, buoyed with all the good wishes, feeling mentally strong and loved. I was sure it wouldn't be as bad as I feared. I carried a copy of Siddhartha Mukherjee's biography of cancer: *The Emperor of All*

Maladies. The idea of reading about chemo, while getting it, was meta and cool.

I didn't make it past the first page. The chemo was preceded by 'premedications,' a combination of an antiemetic and an antihistamine, to prevent nausea or an allergic reaction, because—gasp, why had no one ever told me?—some people go into anaphylactic shock on receiving chemo. I didn't, but the antihistamine knocked me into a fevered sleep that tended to last the duration of the whole session—usually about an hour and a half in total.

Getting the chemo was painless, thanks to the PICC line. Mostly I just felt as though someone was gradually stuffing my cranium with cotton wool. There was a sense of hibernation, of wintering, of turning slow and inward. Sometimes it took a long time for me to muster the energy to reach out and press the bell that summoned the nurse to inform her the bag of drugs had dripped dry. That I could now go home. The chemo chair had become an almost talismanic object of horror for me. I certainly did not want to stay in it, but often even that felt preferable to moving.

EC's landscape, for the most part, was bleak. The predominant climate was nausea, punctuated with occasional vomiting. The gastronomy consisted antiemetic pills and daily injections of filgrastim—a drug that replenished my decimated white blood cells enough for the oncologist to declare me able to withstand the next infusion. My hair fell out on schedule, during the second cycle. I had my last ever period that same week.

It was in EC that my pregnancies felt closest. In both these landscapes, my arms became practised at embracing the toilet. Chemo brought on nausea, muscle aches, brittle nails, fatigue, the narrowing of life to a focus on the physical. But these were no strangers. They'd been by a couple of times before, once with my older son and once with the younger.

It took me about eight days after each infusion to start feeling better. But the blessed days between recovery and the next chemo were possibly the most pleasurable I've experienced. To feel not nauseous after days of a stomach in spasm was deeply joyous. There was an almost absurd happiness to be had in taking a walk in the park on a fine day, or having a warm bath on a cold one, when the memory of being able to do neither was still fresh. The negative gratification of the lack of pain, the absence of nausea, the removal of needles from one's veins, was more profound than gratifications unleavened by difficulty. It was like the difference between drinking a glass of water because it's handy and downing one after you've been trudging, dehydrated, through a desert. The absence of thirst that follows its prolonged presence is ambrosial.

On recovery days, I worked, writing columns with a clarity that was self-aware of its transience, and more crystal for that knowledge. I also travelled every weekend before an infusion—to Seville, to Valencia, to Extremadura. I went to the ballet. I met with friends. I ate. I danced with my boys. I sucked up every minute of the precious time before it was back to the Chair.

And even on the bad days, there was the family bed, the corner of EC that I spent most time in. What a place of plenitude this bed was, heaped with cats and children, and books piled up by the side. When I was too tired to talk, I communicated with those who joined me there through cuddles. It sustained me, that bed. It allowed me to endure.

The terrain was rough, but I trudged on. And eventually, the trough gave way to another part of the kingdom—a place called the Middle. It was still in Chemo, but in the locality of taxanes, with the anthracyclines blessedly behind me. This area had a quasi, third place quality about it. I journeyed here with quasi-normal levels of energy. I'd become quasi-fluent in Oncolish. And by now I, was only in quasi-shock at the unexpected journey I found myself on.

The Taxol infusions were weekly. They left me tired for about a day and then quasi-well for the rest of the week. The effect was cumulative, though, so that I was a lot more fatigued by infusion number eight than I had been after number one. I also developed mild neuropathy—a sensation of pins and needles—in my fingers and toes. My nails turned black. My eyelashes, which had clung to the eyelids for months, finally lost the battle and fell off. But compared to EC, this was a quasi-hoot.

I could now see past the border of the kingdom of the sick, beyond which the home I'd grown up in, the kingdom of the well, shimmered seductively. But it was during this period that I made a choice to focus on the quasi-shitty present, rather than fixating on what lay beyond, because I knew by now, at a visceral level, how illusionary the beyond was.

Nowhere is wholly bad. I can say this for a fact, having lived in nine countries, ten if you include the kingdom of the sick. Beijing had bad air, but great food. Brussels was boring, but its weekend farmer's markets were fabulous. Jakarta's traffic was hellish, but the people stuck in the gridlock were so sweet-tempered. Tokyo's garbage recycling rules were enough to reduce the toughest among us to tears, but spring's cherry blossoms could compensate for virtually any annoyance.

The kingdom of the sick wasn't easy to appreciate. It lacked much in the way of physical comfort, bodily autonomy, hair. Yet it was home to cats, music, anaesthesia, health insurance and guilt-free Netflix binging. Luckily, my right arm and pectoral muscles, the more important ones for right-handed me, were unaffected. My tumour had been a leftie. It was also winter, which meant the PICC-line was covered up by clothes, and in general, less uncomfortable than it would have been in the sweaty summer. I had been diagnosed post-pandemic and spared the need to weigh the pros and cons of possibly dying from COVID vs cancer. The gratitude was profound.

Nonetheless, the longer I spent in the Middle, the more I realised that a part of me was behaving like a refugee, fixated on the idea of return to the safety of home. But the closer I got to the border, the clearer a disorienting truth became. The kingdom of the well that I had spied shimmering on the other side wasn't just being seductive. Its shimmer revealed its true nature as a mirage. There was nothing quasi about this truth.

Sontag said we were all born with dual citizenship to the kingdoms of the well and the sick. But as I walked through the in-between of the Middle, I increasingly felt she was wrong. In fact, there is only one place, and one passport—to the kingdom of life. A land whose one irreducible certainty is death. We begin dying from the moment we are born. Some of us are dying faster than others, but there is no safety in going 'home.' We die in every kingdom. It's the universal finishing line.

I read *The Art of Dying* by Peter Schjeldahl, head art critic of the *New Yorker*. It was one of his last pieces before he passed, of lung cancer. 'Life doesn't go on. It goes nowhere except away. Death goes on,' he wrote. 'Going on is what death does for a living.'

It could seem a tad unsavoury, all this talk of death, given the efforts modern cultures make to ignore it. Death makes us shifty. We want to type in 'RIP' on the social media announcement and hurriedly move on to 'staying blessed'. But in the Middle, I stopped being shifty, coming alive to my being alive, a state that necessarily entailed my death. The realisation was exegetic, like travels in new countries tend to be. All manner of clichés—from *carpe diem* to stopping to smell the roses—no longer seemed trite. Their veracity was the flora of the Middle's long valley.

In taxane territory, the weather was less turbulent. It calmed from oxygen-masks-dropping-panic-&-pray levels, to a fasten-your-seatbelts-and-refrain-from-visiting-the-lavatories stage. I spent much time contemplating the strange nature of time—how it could both run and stand still, how it was both fungible and irreversible. But in the end, in every avatar, it was simply precious.

Travelling in Cancer, which is as much a part of the kingdom of life as Paris or New Delhi, made me fierce with an awareness about the need to double down on the big questions of what constitutes joy, what to regret and what to discard without it. From this vantage, life Before Cancer almost felt anaesthetised. It had been less painful, in both literal and metaphorical ways, but also less vital.

To return to the sakura, apposite given how travelling often leaves us with a sense of having come full circle, if we are lucky, our life is like the cherry blossom. We blaze in brief beauty. If not, we are like the cicadas of Japan's high summer: noisy, unloved and very soon—dead.

As Matsuo Bashō's haiku says of these gossamer-winged cockroaches:

> Nothing in the cry
> of cicadas suggests they
> are about to die.

In the kingdom of life, the trick is to live meaningfully every day, with death whispering at your neck. It's quite a trick.

It is November 2023. I am forty-eight years old. I clamber up on the coffee table, a tad unsteady in my high heels. A drop of champagne spills from the flute I'm clutching. This has been a birthday party to remember. I raise the glass in a toast, 'To life,' I say, feeling ridiculously joyful, 'L'chaim!'

3

LANGUAGE

Foreigners, to whom the tongue is strange, have us at a disadvantage. The Chinese must know better the sound of Antony and Cleopatra than we do.

Virginia Woolf

The sound of a language is where it all begins.

Ursula Le Guin

It is late fall in 2002. I am twenty-seven years old and failing to ask for a sachet of sugar to add to my coffee. The waitress persistently points to photos of assorted soups on the menu. '*Wo* (I) *yao* (want) *tang* (sugar),' I try, once again, in my freshly learnt Mandarin. 'Tang,' she repeats, nodding her head in agreement, while pointing to the soups. We gape at each other like a pair of blowfish. It's an impasse. Journeying in new languages is full of these.

Chinese is a non-alphabetic idiom, more visual—all dashes, dots and lines—than the phonic varieties that use 'abc's or the like. When a Chinese person cannot understand what someone else is saying, they don't spell it out, but use their index finger to draw it in the air, the sense impression of the strokes lingering a while in the ether.

The alphabets of the two languages that I grew up speaking, English and Hindi have twenty-six and forty-five letters, respectively. These letters are pure sound and only form meaning when combined into words. In contrast, Chinese logograms are called characters, and each one is an amalgamation of meaning and sound. There are more than 1,00,000 different characters in this scriptural universe, although to be considered reasonably literate, you need to know 'only' between 3,000 and 6,000.

The tang-tang tussle the waitress and I are having has to do with the inordinate number of homonyms, or characters that are represented by the same sound—so that they are spelt in the same way in their standardised alphabetic form, called Pinyin.

The Pinyin spelling of 'yi,' for instance, is shared by nearly 200 characters, including ones that mean 'one,' 'cloth,' 'to lean,' 'she,' 'ripple,' 'a squeal' and so on. What distinguishes them—albeit only to an extent—is the tone in which they are enunciated.

Tang in what is called the first tone (a high, flat one) is soup, while *tang* in the second tone, (a rising one, as if asking a question) is sugar. If I could have squiggled 糖 in the air like a local, instead of verbalising it with the wrong tone, no one would have thought I meant soup, 汤.

Learning Chinese in Pinyin, as I am, as most foreigners do, has severe limitations. A friend tells me the story of a celebrated linguist, Zhao Yuanren, who set out to demonstrate the inadequacies of Pinyin. He composed a ninety-two-character story using thirty-one different characters about a man called Shi who mistakenly tried to eat ten lions carved from stone.

This is how it reads in Chinese:

> 石室诗士施氏，嗜狮，誓食十狮。
> 氏时时适市视狮。
> 十时，适十狮适市。
> 是时，适施氏适市。
> 氏视是十狮，恃矢势，使是十狮逝世。

氏拾是十狮尸，适石室。
石室湿，氏使侍拭石室。
石室拭，氏始试食是十狮。
食时，始识是十狮尸，实十石狮尸。
试释是事。

But this is how it would be alphabetised in Pinyin:

Shī Shì shí shī shī
Shíshì shīshì Shī Shì, shì shī, shì shí shí shī.
Shì shíshí shì shì shì shī.
Shí shí, shì shí shī shì shṅ.
Shì shí, shì Shī Shì shì shì.
Shì shì shì shí shī, shì shī shì, shī shì shí shī shìshì.
Shì shí shì shí shī shī, shì shíshì.
Shíshì shī, Shì shī shì shì shíshì.
Shíshì shì, Shì shī shì shí shì shí shī.
Shí shí, shī shí shì shí shī shī, shí shí shí shī shī.
Shì shì shì shì.

Finally, here it is in English translation:

The Lion-Eating Poet in the Stone Den
In a stone den was a poet called *Shi Shi*, who was a lion addict and had resolved to eat ten lions.
He often went to the market to look for lions.
At ten o'clock, ten lions had just arrived at the market.
At that time, Shi had just arrived at the market.
He saw those ten lions and, using his trusty arrows, caused the ten lions to die.
He brought the corpses of the ten lions to the stone den.
The stone den was damp. So, he asked his servants to wipe it.
After wiping the stone den, he tried to eat those ten lions.
When he ate, he realised that these ten lions were, in fact, ten stone lion corpses.
Try to explain this matter.

Pinyin helps me communicate at a basic level, but being unable to rely on script is akin to an amputation of the most foundational block of sense-making. Scriptural skill is what gave my Brahmin forefathers their status, their arrogant sense of self. But in Beijing, I am illiterate, angootha chaap. The result is an almost permanent state of bafflement, but also one of full attention, neurons firing.

I walk around the city and really look at how people hold themselves and how they laugh. How they size up worth and how they bite into candied crab apples. Without script, I am decentred. The least interesting person in any conversation, utterly ignorable. It is from the periphery that I watch, infer, and learn.

My presence in China surprises me when I pause to think about it. It had never been part of any plan. And yet, here I am, just as the hibernating 'dragon' that had long been prophesied to make the world tremble upon awakening, is doing just that, belching infernos of skyscrapers and artificial Christmas trees. I learn that about 70 per cent of the world's Christmas ornaments are 'Made in China'. Ditto for sex toys and metallic lighters.

Being here is the result of an accident of the heart. A young man I met while at graduate school in London was convinced that we were in an epochal phase in world history, headlined by the rise of China. And so, I followed him here—a Spaniard, whom I will go on to marry—to this frantic city with its street sizzle and jackhammering auralscape. To this Kingdom of Characters, where half the buildings are on death row, marked with 拆 – the character for 'tear down,' (pronounced *chai* in first tone). Beijing is being demolished and reconstructed at a pace difficult for the human brain to absorb. It is easy to lose one's bearings here.

I teach news writing in English at a university called the Beijing Broadcasting Institute, to over 200 pupils. On the first day of class, student after student stood up and introduced themselves with their 'English' names. There was a Byron and an Ice. One boy was called Victoria, and another went by 'Fat' ('because, I am fat,' he'd added by way of explanation).

I discover that adopting Western monikers for use when interacting with foreigners is standard practice in China. Initially, I'd been uncomfortable with this forced anglicisation. I had always insisted on being called Pallavi while studying in the UK, braving mispronunciations that ranged from Pavalova to Pullover, and denying those who would rechristen me 'Polly'. I'd thought it to be a matter of global equity. Why should an Indian name be made easier for a Westerner to pronounce? Erstwhile colonisers had already taken so much from us. I was determined to refuse them my name.

This was before I began to frequent Starbucks and became more practical-minded—an age-related hazard. (These days I live in Spain and go by Maria Jose at restaurants and hair salons.)

But also, name changing was a two-way lane in China. Being logographic meant that Chinese could not absorb sounds that were absent from its character-based script, a script that was as aurally poor as it was visually rich. The tens of thousands of extant Chinese characters only had 420 different corresponding sounds. The result: it was impossible to say Elizabeth or Pallavi in Chinese; there were no characters with analogous sound combinations.

And so, I become Ai Bei. My students helped me choose the name. Ai (because it is pronounced like the first syllable of my family name, Aiyar) and Bei (because, like Pallavi, it means flower bud).

At the time of the sugar-soup muddle, I hadn't lived in China for long. Less than a year. But already, Ai Bei was different from Pallavi. Travel, when done well, is always transformative in ways both big and small. And I'd been travelling in both Chinese and China—a double metamorphosis.

Unlike Pallavi, Ai Bei knows how to hide sea slugs behind a mound of rice, to avoid giving offence at turning down an expensive treat at a banquet. She isn't startled by students talking to trees with exaggerated enunciation. This is how they perfect their broadcast accents before TV job interviews. She has learned to avoid iced water at any cost. And when people tell Ai Bei that Mao Zedong had been 70 per cent correct and 30 per cent wrong in his actions, unlike Pallavi, who'd been impressed by such considered quantification, Ai Bei is aware that this is merely rote regurgitation of the official Chinese Communist Party's assessment of their erstwhile Chairman.

At the restaurant, I finally get sugar for my coffee and am able to move on to the food items on the menu. Amidst the more prosaic items, there is something called 'Fuck the exploded duck.' Pallavi would have been nonplussed by this unlikely-sounding dish, but Ai Bei's wanderings in Chinese have paid off. She is learning to understand what is meant, rather than what is said.

The problem, as ever, when it comes to Chinese-English translations is homonyms. The pinyin word 'gan' can mean both 'dry' and 'to do'. The latter is also a colloquialism for 'fuck'. In Beijing, I find numerous iterations of this particular mistranslation. At a local supermarket, the dry food aisle is labelled 'assorted fuck'. On another menu, in another restaurant, a spicy stir fry of green vegetables and dried tofu is described in English as, 'benumbed hot vegetables fries fuck silk'.

Beijing is gearing up to host the 2008 Olympic Games. And the authorities have decided that to be global necessitates being clothed in English. Worries about the ability of the Chinese language to accommodate the demands of modernity have a storied intellectual history. But in this moment, there are English signs and hoardings everywhere in the capital city. They are intended to signal openness to the outside world.

I am enthralled by these. I realise that in travelling from one language to another, there is something that is lost, yes, but even more that is laid bare. There is a directness, shorn of any euphemistic nuance, that makes the translations searingly accurate. In one hospital, I find a sign on a door that reads 'vagina examination room.' At a busy traffic intersection, another hospital is heralded by an enormous hoarding proclaiming, Dongda Hospital for Anus and Intestine Disease. (In 2007, the sign is eventually 'corrected' to 'Dongda Hospital of Proctology'.)

The adjective 'civilized' is attached to all manner of things. Airports are declared to be 'civilized airports,' and neighbourhoods claim the same for themselves. A 'civilized' place, I learn to understand, is one where people act with '*wenming*,' or sophisticated manners: they do not spit, they do form orderly queues.

In our own languages, we have the kind of topographical competence that allows us to obscure and reveal simultaneously. But when travelling in a new linguistic landscape, such cleverness becomes difficult. We are forced to be direct, shorn of polish, wholly our flawed, stuttering selves.

In China, everyone speaks Chinese, and I am asked, repeatedly, about what Indian is like.[1] I dread the question because it has such a convoluted answer: 'There is no such language. We have almost two dozen official languages: Hindi, Tamil, Punjabi, Bengali to name a few. English is an Indian language too ... etc.' At the conclusion of this yarn, people look at me with an admixture of bewilderment and pity.

There was a time when the ignorance of my interlocutor in assuming 'Indian' to be a language bothered me. But in China, there is this other thing that I feel the need to grapple with—the fact that I am Indian in English. My physical home is India, but my linguistic one is English. I grew up speaking English with my parents; it is in English that I dream and in which I speak to my dog. It all seemed quite unremarkable when I was a child, but here in Beijing, it increasingly feels, if not wrong, at least something that deserves interrogation.

The bond between language and identity is profound. So, what does it mean for an Indian to have lost her 'native' languages? In my case, my first language is neither my mother's tongue of Hindi, nor Tamil, my father's. I attended an 'English-medium' school in Delhi where everything, except Hindi, was taught in English. I understand Hindi well enough, although it is an oral, rather than a literary, language for me. I *can* read in Hindi, but only haltingly, at primary-school level. This is because I *don't* read in Hindi.

I had spoken Hindi daily while growing up, but exclusively to the 'servants' or other non-English speaking Indians: shopkeepers, autorickshaw drivers, security guards at the school gates, and random people on the street I'd needed to ask for directions. Non-English-speaking Indians—an overwhelming majority—had been but a cast of supporting characters in the play where I occupied centre stage.

India's polyphony allowed for this state of affairs. We have twenty-two official languages and almost as many mother tongues as gods. But although all languages are equal, some are patently more equal than others. Ultimately, there is one linguistic fault line that really matters. The one between English and non-English. Only 0.02 per cent of Indians speak English as their first language.[2] And yet, English is the language of the supreme court, of much of government, of the media at the national level, of elite business—and of success. Indians have many ways to divide themselves: by religion, diet, colour, gender. But the English–non-English divide creates the most rarefied distinction of all. In India, English is not just a language, it is a caste, one that is implicated in a smorgasbord of inequalities.

As a child, I hadn't felt alienated from, or alien in, India. I was proud of my country's linguistic diversity and had no doubts about my authenticity as an Indian. I believed India wonderfully unique in its resistance to the policing of its definition. There was no authority that could decide who was truly Indian or not. My idea of the nation was as valid as yours.

Jawaharlal Nehru, India's first Prime Minister, famously described India (in superb English) as an 'ancient palimpsest on which layer upon layer of thought and reverie had been inscribed, and yet no succeeding layer had completely hidden or erased what had been written previously.' Ergo, an English-Indian like me was as valid as any other sort.

What's more, my generation had decolonised the language, domesticated it. I inhabited Englishness with less pathos than the generation who'd actually been taught by Englishmen at school. My accent was free of stuffiness, my consonants unapologetically Indian-hard, and my vowels free of striving for some sliced-cucumber-sandwich ideal. Mine was an English unselfconsciously peppered with 'acchas' and 'chalos' and 'yaars'. It was breathable and loose, like a sari—not buttoned up in a suit and tie.

English was India's lingua franca. It allowed for Hindi-influenced northerners and the Dravidian language speakers in the south to communicate. My mother and father could not have fallen in love and birthed me, had it not been for the linguistic bridge of English.

But here in China, some of these arguments lose their Oxford-Union debate sheen. It is true that India is a palimpsest and has absorbed cultural influences from elsewhere to make them her own. But unlike the Mughals and their descendants who stayed and became Indian—so that Urdu is as 'authentically' Indian as turmeric—the British (and their language) always remained a race apart. Of India's 1.4 billion people, only between 1,25,000-1,50,000 are Anglo-Indian or Indians with some English ancestry.

And while English-Indians like me have domesticated the language, our playful bending of the idiom—exemplified by literary stars like Salman Rushdie and Arundhati Roy—is of a different register to the aspiring Indian-English of the great majority of India's English speakers. Most of my compatriots don't joyfully experiment with the language as much as desperately try, and often fail, to gain a modicum of fluency in it. The language many learn is syntactically wrong and badly pronounced. It can have an air of desperation about it: as a ticket to an imagined life of plenty. English may connect India, but it also disconnects it.

Language has a profound impact on the way in which we render our reality. And the fact that mine, English, is inescapably mediated through the colonial gaze is an uncomfortable one. It has taken living in China, another large, populous, developing Asian country, to force me to contend with this. Travelling is as much about the places you visit as it is about the place you have left behind. It interrogates the taken-for-granted notion of home. It holds up a mirror to what you thought of as 'normal,' and perhaps helps you discard the concept altogether.

Ai Bei knows not to think of veg/non-veg as the normal manner of categorising food. She's discovered it isn't abnormal to walk backwards while slapping at your rib cage in parks. And she has learnt it isn't normal to have to conjugate verbs to indicate tense. In Mandarin, there is no I go, I went, I will go. Instead, there is only 'I go' with time references attached: I go, I go yesterday, I go tomorrow. Grammar, she is realising, is not the only way to make language intelligible. There is a plenitude of valid ways of being.

By 2006, Beijing is a foreigner to the city I had first encountered in 2002. I interview the mayor for a story I am writing on preparations for the 2008 Olympic Games and learn that the physical transformations of the city are so great that the municipality has taken to issuing new maps every three months. The mayor laughs queasily while telling me this. I am stunned.

Later that day, I sip a cup of chrysanthemum tea outside a café, looking on as a group of pepper pot-haired women perform a fan dance routine in front of a gigantic pile of rubble–the remnants of their recently demised housing block. I wonder how the older generation in China preserves their sense of identity, given the epochal transformations that have been squeezed into their brief lives.

One of the neighbours in the Beijing alleyway that I live in is a ninety-year-old lady called Lao Tai Tai or 'Old Mrs'. Her face is laced with a maze of fine lines, but it's her miniature feet that draw my attention. Starting from the age of six, the bones in her feet were repeatedly broken and bent to achieve impossibly tiny, deformed, 'lotus feet'. These were once the standard of beauty in China, akin to the modern-day Brazilian butt lift. Foot binding was officially banned in 1912, although only really stamped out after the communist accession in 1949.

Lao Tai Tai tells me that she had moved to Beijing from a village in Shandong province in 1946. I become vertiginous at the thought of someone having lived through imperial China's morphing into a communist country, and then witnessing the capricious horrors of Mao's mass campaigns give way to the capitalist excesses of the twenty-first century. How could anyone process all of this? How did one maintain a personal narrative arc that was not as violently fractured as the broader political canvas against which this life had played out?

China's written language is the key. Having survived the battering ram of history, it is characters, more than religion or architecture or climate, that have held the country together. Physical buildings in China rarely survive very long—the result of fires, wars, natural disasters and 'upgradation'. But Chinese characters have remained largely unchanged for 2,200 years. By comparison, the number of letters in the Roman alphabet were in flux until the sixteenth century, when 'j' split from 'i' and completed the twenty-six-letter English alphabet currently in use.[3]

There is something sacred about the written word in China, underscored by the cultural reverence accorded to calligraphy.

Handwriting, in the erstwhile Middle Kingdom, was accorded more artistic respect than painting or sculpture. How you wrote was as important as what you wrote.

Flicking through the People's Daily newspaper has become a habit, so that I encounter the most reproduced example of calligraphy in the country every day: the four character phrase, *Ren min Ri bao*, (The People's Daily), originally penned by Chairman Mao. That calligraphy survived as a practice under the communists, even as they sought to destroy other elite cultural markers from religion to literature, is revealing.[4]

It is in its spoken form that Chinese has seen more changes. Until relatively recently there was no 'Chinese,' just as there is no 'Indian'. The Communist Party, helmed by Mao, pushed for Putonghua, a newly standardised idiom based on the language spoken in the nation's capital, Beijing, to become what we now refer to as 'Chinese'. This took considerable political manoeuvring to achieve.

Prior to the 1950s, Han Chinese people spoke nine main tongues that were mutually unintelligible. These included Mandarin—the basis for Putonghua; Wu (which includes Shanghainese); Xiang; Gan; Jin; Kejia; Yue; Northern Min; and Southern Min, each with many sub-dialects. Non-Han peoples spoke an additional 300-odd languages including Mongolian, Tibetan, Uyghur and Zhuang.

Making Putonghua (literally—the common speech) the national language, was intended to help consolidate state power, facilitate communication between the diverse citizenry and to promote literacy. But despite Mao's backing, it took until 1982, when a revised constitution was promulgated, for Putonghua (the Mandarin Chinese of today) to officially secure its place as the standard national language.

It is mid-2011. I am thirty-five and newly arrived in Indonesia. It is a difficult time. I am stuck in a cramped, temporary accommodation with my Beijing-born four-year-old and Brussels-sprouted fifteen-month baby, two disoriented cats and not much help. The Spaniard who had waxed eloquent about the rise of China is now my husband. He has disappeared into office and adult life, while I desperately try to find playgroups, schools and a permanent home.

There is a jigsaw-like quality to the first few months in any new country, as in a new language. Observations become meaningful in non-contiguous snatches, like the scattered pieces of a puzzle. I'm a small child again, watching letters transform from two-dimensional shapes into signifiers with wells of expression.

The first thing that strikes me is the improbability of the names in this country. Scanning the newspaper on any given day unveils a tasting-menu of monikers, shaken and stirred into exotic cocktails: Teddy Anwar, Wisnu Ali, Leanardus Nyoman, Muhammad Krisna, Batman Bin Suparman.[5]

This surfeit of diversity makes for a stark contrast from the problem of paucity that Chinese nomenclature had suffered from. Over 85 per cent of China's then 1.3 billion people shared hundred family names. China was home to subnations of 93 million 'Wangs' and 92 million 'Lis.' The word for the 'common man' in Chinese was, '*laobaixing*', literally the 'old 100 names'—a reference to the hundred names that make up the overweening majority of Han Chinese surnames. Until a few decades ago, school children across China were taught to reel off a list of these by rote: 'Zhao, Qian, Sun, Li, Zhou, Wu, Zheng, Wang,' began the nursery rhyme-like inventory.

The predicament of this appellative dearth has been aggravated by the tendency of Chinese parents to follow naming fashions, so that a large number of children in particular generations ended up with not only the same family names, but also identical personal ones. Cohorts of children in the 1960s and 1970s, for example, were called *Guo Qin* (National Day), *Wei Hong* (Protect Communism) and *Wen Ge* (Cultural Revolution), as parents attempted to demonstrate their patriotic credentials. In contrast, while teaching at the Beijing Broadcasting Institute, I'd barely been able to move without bumping into a *Mei* (beautiful) or *Yin* (elegant).

A bank clerk friend, Ms Song, once told me about two colleagues with the same name: Wang Qiang. The two were differentiated in the standard Chinese way, by adding the prefix 'lao,' older, or 'xiao,' younger, to their names. But this method didn't always work. 'Once we heard that Wang Qiang was transferring to our department. We were all happy. But in fact, it was the other Wang Qiang. That one had bad body odour, so we were less happy,' Song had recounted.

In Jakarta, I struggle to detect any method to the chaos of names. Some people go by one, others by ten. Monikers derive from Sanskrit, Arabic, local languages, western pop culture and the fertile imagination of parents. A top defence lawyer is called Hotman Paris Hutapea, a prominent oligarch, Garibaldi Thorir. The jihadist minister for religious affairs, accused of embezzling state funds allocated for the haj pilgrimage, is Suryadharma Ali. I read an article about someone called 'Andi Go To School'. Goto (Andi Go To School's diminutive form), is a policeman from Central Java. His father, also possessed of an unusual appellation—Bullking—named his son thus, in the hope that it would make Andi love going to school.

Travelling in Bahasa Indonesia is eclectic and crowded, like the country itself. And for me, an Indian, it is full of familiar echoes. Much of the language is based on Sanskrit, the root of several Indian idioms and one that I'd studied desultorily in middle school. It's a language I associate with the kind of archaic speech that mythological characters use in TV renditions of Hindu epics. But in Jakarta, shop attendants and itinerant street vendors pepper ordinary conversation with lofty (to an Indian) vocabulary like 'manushya' (man), 'karena' (because) and 'gajah' (elephant)—the equivalent of being 'thee'd and 'thou'd for an English speaker.

The word 'bahasa' itself is a derivative of the Sanskrit term for language, 'bhasha'. But other than Sanskrit, Indonesia's linguistic cosmos is crammed with loanwords from Persian, Arabic and European tongues. I gather nouns and adjectives with some ease: utara (north), masjid (mosque), roti (bread), asli (genuine), stroberi (strawberry), konferensi (conference), dunia (world), anggur (grape). It is a cinch for an English-Indian like me.

But India and Indonesia do not merely share similar sounding names. Our cultures and histories are deeply intertwined. Our civilisations have proved capacious, open to similar, amalgamative influences. Hindu, Buddhist, Animist, Islamic and Christian thought and practices have mingled in complex historical patterns. Pilgrims, traders, warriors and colonisers from Arabia, Persia, China and Europe have left imprints on both countries. '*Bhinekka Tinggal Ika*' (multiple but one), Indonesia's Sanskrit-tinged national motto, is in essence identical to modern India's ideal of 'Unity in Diversity.'

Like India, Indonesia is home to hundreds of languages, many of which do not share scripts or linguistic roots. But like China, independent Indonesia adopted a single national language: Bahasa Indonesia. This took an act of social engineering considerably more complicated than that of the casting of Putonghua as Chinese.

Bahasa is, in fact, a form of Malay. At the time of Indonesia's independence in 1947, it was neither the language of the majority, nor of the political elite.[6] These labels belonged to Javanese. Java was Indonesia's most populous island and the centre of gravity of its nationalist movement. Bypassing Javanese in favour of the newly minted Bahasa Indonesia, literally the 'language of Indonesia,' was an unusual decision.

Malay had long been a lingua franca, the argot of traders across Southeast Asia. It was officially adopted by the Indonesian nationalist movement in 1928, by which time it had already emerged as a rallying symbol of resistance to colonialism. The reason Malay was able to perform this role was in part due to the absence of a Dutch equivalent to Macaulay—the man who introduced English-language education in India. Under Dutch rule, 'native' Indonesians were discouraged from learning the language of their colonial masters, so that unlike English in India, Dutch was not a lubricant for the development of a nationalist consciousness.

Indonesian nationalists, including those from Java, were keenly aware of the complex plurality that they were attempting to knit into a coherent unity. They determined therefore, not to conflate their emergent sense of nationhood with any single ethnicity or religion. Hence the retrofitting of a minority tongue, Malay, into the national language: the Bahasa Indonesia of today. It also helped that Bahasa was a simple and flexible idiom, one that had soaked up loan words from divergent cultural milieux. It had a no-fuss grammar and was written in the Roman script.

On a rainy August afternoon, I meet with Goenawan Mohamad, one of Indonesia's leading public intellectuals. Goenawan is an orthographical variation of Gunawan, a Sanskritic Hindu name that means 'someone gifted with an abundance of good qualities'. He is handsome in a grizzly way; the air of a smoker about him.

Goenawan exhales meditatively before responding to my query about the importance of Bahasa, the language he writes in, to Indonesian identity. Javanese was eschewed as a national language because that choice would have signalled too close an identification of Indonesia with Java, he confirms. It would have defeated the nationalist aim of unifying the archipelago's 17,000 islands. But there was an additional reason, he says. Javanese is a deeply hierarchical language; one imbued with feudal terminology. It is linguistically antithetical to modernity's ideals of citizenship and egalitarianism. For instance, the Javanese speaker must use forms of address that identify her social ranking in relation to the person being addressed.

In India, a quip-turned-received-wisdom claims that Bollywood and cricket are the glue that binds the country together. In Indonesia, that function unequivocally belongs to Bahasa. 'Without Bahasa, we could not have survived. There would be no Indonesia without Indonesian,' says Goenawan, stubbing out his cigarette, a gesture that lends his conclusion emphasis.

At Indonesian independence, only 5 per cent of the population used Bahasa routinely. Several decades down the line, and 94 per cent of the country speak it. Yet even today, only about 20 million of the country's 270 million citizens speak it as a first language. In contrast, Javanese is spoken by upwards of 70 million as a mother tongue. Sundanese, by 25 million.

There is an unusual dichotomy between the spoken and written word here. When they write, Indonesians do so almost uniformly in Bahasa Indonesia. There hasn't been a daily newspaper in Javanese for decades. Literature is also invariably written in Indonesian. But spoken languages are rich in diversity. In this disconnection between the written and oral worlds, Indonesia's linguistic geography mirrors that of China's. In both nations, the former is centripetal, the latter, centrifugal—with the countries constructed in the balance.

India's land of Babel is the odd one out. Not that the country did not have its share of single national-language promoters. The quest for a 'rashtra bhasha,' or national language in India, was turbulent. The constitutional assembly held meetings between 1947 and 1950, tasked with the formidable assignment of thrashing out a modern constitution for an ancient civilisation that was now being thrust into a liberal-secular future. Debates raged around which language should be spoken in assembly meetings and which one should be used to write the constitution itself.

When assembly member R.V. Dhulker, moved an amendment while speaking in Hindustani, (the Urdu-infused Hindi that was the dominant tongue of the north including the capital, Delhi) assembly Chairman Rajendra Prasad, was unimpressed. Prasad reprimanded Dhulker, reminding him that many of those present struggled to understand Hindustani. To this Dhulker replied:

> People who do not know Hindustani have no right to stay in India. People who are present in this House to fashion a constitution for India and do not know Hindustani are not worthy to be members of this assembly.

Eventually, it was recommended that 'Hindustani, written either in Devanagari or the Persian script at the option of the citizen, shall, as the national language, be the first official language of the Union. English shall be the second official language for such period as the Union may, by law, determine.'

But even as independent India matured into adolescence and beyond, it proved impossible to implement this goal. Hindi/Hindustani was never declared a national language. Instead, along with English, it remains an official language, almost eighty years on. The original idea was for English to be unhyphenated from Hindi, demitting its official role after an interim period of fifteen years. But the thought of Hindi monopolising India caused large-scale protests in the southern part of the country, a region whose Dravidian languages had scant fraternal feelings for their northern compatois. In the south, the idea of Hindi as a national language was tantamount to northern linguistic imperialism.

Ultimately, the Official Languages Act of 1963 was passed by the Indian Parliament, which guaranteed that both Hindi and English would continue to be used for official purposes, indefinitely. In addition, several regional languages were also recognised as 'scheduled', entitled to representation in the Official Language Commission. There were upwards of twenty of these at the time that I lived in China.

And so it was that I came from a country with no national language, two official ones and more than a score 'scheduled' tongues. I had grown up, thinking this to be unremarkable. It was all I'd known. But learning about the divergent linguistic paths that large and plural Asian nations like China and Indonesia had chosen brought India's embrace of cacophony over idiomatic homogeneity into sharp relief. It forced me to examine this choice more critically.

I had always believed India to have avoided balkanisation because it had eschewed a national idiom. The idea that a nation needs a national language is entrenched in the nineteenth-century European model, but in India's case, allowing a multiplicity of tongues, arguably strengthened the state's political viability. It was an unusual decision, to focus on diversity as the basis for the nation's unifying glue. Yet, it had worked.

However, travels in languages outside of India also made me less quick to dismiss the proponents of 'Indian' or a single rashtra bhasha. National language enthusiasts tended to live within the over-wrought nationalistic Right, a place located at such distance from my ideological, liberal-left home, that growing up, I hadn't even heard their arguments.

But of what good is travel if it doesn't make the traveller rethink long-held assumptions? Over the years, I became able to look upon India's linguistic paradigm through new, and bemused, eyes. These were the eyes of my puzzled Chinese and Indonesian interlocuters who remained unconvinced by the state of linguistic affairs in India, despite my best attempts to justify them.

The paths to developing a common language in both China and Indonesia had not been pothole-free. Yet they had terminated in tangible benefits, ranging from literacy to the fostering of a sense of commonality. Journeying in Bahasa

Indonesia, in particular, had me imagining alternative futures for India, in which Indians shared a language, one that was neither the imperial tongue of English nor that of the majority, Hindi. Our founding fathers had opted for polyphony on the grounds of our diversity, but an archipelago like Indonesia was also vertiginously plural.

Travelling holds up a mirror to the familiar, to what has become invisible because of its quotidian nature. It does not always, or even often, provide answers. But it does raise uncomfortable questions. And so, I remain conflicted on the matter of India's linguistic effervescence. But what I know is that when it comes to languages and nations, there is no one-size-fits-all solution. Tongues are tangled and troublesome.

Just how troublesome, is something I'd first learned in the tiny, often overlooked, western European country of Belgium, a land roiled by language like no other.

It is 2010 and I am thirty-six years old. It's been hundreds of days since the country I live in last had a government. There are large numbers of unshaven men in front of me. Some sip from cans of beer. The general atmosphere is one of beardly bonhomie, but this is in fact a protest. And the protestors are vowing to stay away from razors until a government is formed. It is funny, and intentionally so, but at the heart of the problem there is language, and in Belgium, language is deadly serious.

I have been resident in Brussels for well over two years and there has been no government in power for much of this time. The country's municipal and city-wide services have scarcely been affected by this lacuna. The garbage is collected regularly; the buses run punctually. But in three days, Belgium will break the dubious world record of the longest period a country has gone without a government, taking over the title from war-torn Iraq. It will have been 250 days since national elections failed to produce a clear winner. Eighty sets of negotiations have taken place since June 2010 to thrash out a compromise between MPs from Flanders, the fiscally conservative and prosperous Dutch-speaking northern half of the country, and Wallonia, the socialist and economically depressed, French-speaking south.

The root of this impasse is language, for all roads in Belgium lead to the Flemish-French face-off that is the global granddaddy of linguistic squabbles.

Since moving to Brussels in early 2009, I've spent a lot of time being confused. I go to meet a friend at the Arts-Loi metro station, but when I exit the subway, the sign says it is the somewhat abusive-sounding Kunst-Wet. Another time, I buy a ticket for Courtrai and come back with one for Kortrijk. The source of this confusion is Brussels' status as an officially bilingual city. Accordingly, all street and direction signs must display names in both French and Dutch.

The reason for this enforced fork-tonguedness? Brussels, Belgium's capital, is the conflicted child of a rocky marriage between Dutch-speaking Flanders and French speaking-Wallonia. Geographically situated in Flanders, the city was historically Dutch-speaking. However, after becoming the capital of Belgium in 1830, it gradually acculturated to the French side of things. In the nineteenth century, 80 per cent of Bruxellois spoke Dutch. By the time the country is about to enter the Guinness Book of World Records for its government-lessness, it is French that is spoken in about 80 per cent of homes.

Usually, a statistic like this is sufficient to clarify the linguistic status quo of a place. But Belgium is a country wracked by language, wrought by language, possessed by language. All data here is seemingly grist for the demagoguery of idiomatic politics. I only need to casually mention the curious linguistic status of Brussels to a local, and they begin to babble irrepressibly. I am told that between 2000 and 2006, the proportion of monolingual Dutch families shrank from 9.5 per cent to 7 per cent.

Linguistic sensitivities are such that language impartiality in Brussels is pushed to absurd extremes. There is a kerfuffle about which should come first on public transport signage, the Flemish or French name. Bus companies cunningly solve the problem by using rotating signs so that offence was avoided. It gets even sillier. Because it proves impossible to find the exact equivalent number of Flemish songs to French, only neutral English, Spanish or Italian songs are piped through in Brussels's metro stations.

In April 2010, the five-party federal coalition government that was in power when I'd first moved to the country collapsed over what sounded like a particularly nasty virus to the uninitiated: the Brussels-Halle-Vilvoorde (BHV) problem. The very same affliction had caused an earlier collapse of the government in 2007, which had left the country without a government for 194 days. The second time around, the no-government situation lasted for 541 days, until December 2011.

What is BHV—this government-toppling scourge? I learn it is but an electoral district where voters have the choice of plumping for either a Dutch- or French-speaking politician. That's it. To understand why this fact has such earth-shattering consequences for Belgian politics I needed to first come to grips with the country's byzantine political system. Belgium, with its grand total of 11 million people and 30,500 square kilometres of territory (by contrast the single Indian state of Madhya Pradesh is spread over 3,08,000 square km and houses about 73 million people) has a dual federal system with six centres of authority.

The Belgian constitution divides all powers between governments for three territorially based regions—Wallonia, Flanders and Brussels—which have separate, directly elected, parliamentary-style legislatures. In addition to the regions, there is a further separation of powers between three disparate communities, which are defined linguistically rather than territorially, comprised of Flemish-, French- and German-speaking groups. It can be difficult to get one's head around. It helps me to think of school history lessons in India and how, under the British Raj, separate electorates were instituted for

Muslims and Hindus. The result was that Muslims could only vote for Muslim candidates and the same for Hindus. And so it is in Belgium, except along linguistic rather than religious lines. There is no national, pan-Belgian constituency. Since the 1960s, all the country's political parties are split into separate French-speaking and Flemish entities. As in the case of Hindus and Muslims under the Raj, Dutch- and French-speakers are unable to cast a 'national' vote, even if they want to.

A citizen can only vote for the candidates on the electoral list linked to her place of residence. A person who lives in Flanders, is in practice, unable to choose a French-speaking candidate, with the reverse holding true for a resident of Wallonia.

Returning to the infamous BHV, a voting district that, while technically in Flanders, had a substantial number of French-speaking residents. In other words, it was an example of an area that belongs to the Flemish *territory* but that has a substantial French *community* resident in it. The electoral rolls for the district did not offer French-speaking candidates, and so francophone residents of the region had been permitted to vote on the electoral lists of nearby Brussels.

The problem? The Flemings didn't like it. Why?

Because they believed such permissiveness would only lead to the creeping French-ification that had already claimed Brussels as francophone—by allowing French speakers to reside in Flemish areas but vote for francophone politicians in Brussels who had little stake in representing Flemish interests. It is over the inability to decide how to split BVH into politically acceptable, linguistically divided, voting regions that Belgium's federal government kept collapsing.

Feeling empathy for Belgium's linguistic squabbling could be difficult. After all, India had managed to weave together more cohesion from far greater plurality, with less melodrama. For a moment, I felt that Belgium represented a failure of generosity; a complete inability to cope with what, from my Indian point of view, was minimal diversity. But the moment did not last.

The more time one spends travelling, the more it dawns how all peoples are united in not only being flawed, but also in being handcuffed to their histories. And it is in this history that the embittered roots of Belgium's linguistic acrimony lay.

From its creation in 1830, a language apartheid was applied in Belgium, where a French-speaking elite in both the southern and northern parts of the country sought to impose French as the sole language of education and government. French, the language of the Belgian aristocracy, came to symbolise everything refined and intelligent, while Dutch, the language of northern peasants, was treated as a coarse country-bumpkin cousin to be kept out of sight.

It wasn't until the Belgian state was fifty years old that the first speech in Dutch was heard in the parliament building in Brussels. The discrimination against Flemish speakers sometimes had tragic consequences. For example, in 1873 a murder trial ended with the wrongful conviction and execution of two Flemings. After their heads had been offed, another person confessed to the crime. It was subsequently found that the defendants could not understand French, that their attorney knew no Dutch, and that the francophone judge had relied on a mistranslation of a conversation overheard by a jailer.

Over the following decades, Dutch speakers painfully clawed back linguistic equality for themselves. But it wasn't a privilege conceded by the haughty French-speaking elite easily. It was only in 1893 that Dutch was recognised as Belgium's second language (although 60 per cent of Belgians used it). In the 1920s, when the University of Ghent was debating becoming exclusively Dutch-speaking, a Walloon MP claimed in all earnestness that replacing French culture with Flemish culture was like 'replacing a lighthouse with a candle.'

There is a point when I am left wondering what makes Belgium a country, in the absence of a tongue. It is writer Luc Sante who provides me an answer in his lyrical, *Factory of Facts*:

> Baked goods. Churches. Weather … Shrubbery. The colour gray … Brickwork…. Silent children, unassertive houseplants … Comic strips … Gherkins … The perpetual imminence of rage, blasphemy, running amok. Trees like fists. Rheumy eyes.

Languages are tricky. They build bridges, but also open up chasms. Travelling in them is always an education.

It is 2020. I am forty-five and my Spanish teacher, who has until now had that practiced look of language instructors around the world—feigned interest in the grammatically mangled, pedestrian utterances of their students—is looking confused. 'Mahatma Gandhi was a what?' she asks, eyes wide. 'An avocado,' I repeat, more hesitantly this time, tipped off by her reaction that I must have said something odd. Again.

I had meant to say 'lawyer,' or '*abogado*' in Spanish, but had ended up saying '*aguacate*' or 'avocado,' no doubt tricked by the French that lingered subterraneously in my overcrowded brain. 'Avocat' referred to both lawyers and the fruit *en français*.

In my mid-forties, I am a serial learner of languages. Not one of those gifted polyglots who effortlessly inhale new tongues as though languorously sucking on a flavoured hookah. I'm more akin to a seriously out-of-shape marathon runner, huffing and hurting, but always with a long way still to go.

Since my years in China, I have spent over a decade in various countries around the world: Belgium, Indonesia, Japan and now, Spain—trying to learn enough of the local languages to avoid embarrassment. It's foolish, of course. Embarrassment is a synonym for learning a new language. And after years of ordering lawyers when I want an avocado salad, I realise that embarrassment is not the most important aspect of the story.

Just as the real value of travelling to a new country is not to take a selfie as proof of enjoyment as to learn about yourself, learning a new language isn't so much about gaining new vocabulary as it is about acquiring empathy for vulnerability.

A consciousness of the privilege bestowed upon you by having access to the right words.

The inability to say interesting things, not think them or know them, but to express them with casual felicity, is an automatic demotion of your perceived value. Lacking the right words strips you of the cultural capital that allows those well-endowed with it to inhabit the world with confidence. Instead, you become diffident, refraining from offering your opinions, not because you don't have them, but because you are ashamed of your pronunciation.

Learning a new language means that you know what it is like to hesitate on the sidelines while others hold centre stage. It is to understand the truth that people who cannot speak 'well' can still be worth listening to. That by making the effort to understand someone who is struggling to express themselves, you do more than a mere kindness to them, you open yourself up to the possibility of learning. The privilege of words is less obvious than material privilege, but is also distorting. Language learning leads to the epiphany that making a mistake is an act of bravery, and the people making them should be patted on the back, not sniggered at.

None of which is to say that we can't enjoy the glorious comedy of mistakes.

A Spanish friend is visibly proud when telling me about how his father had been to jail in the U.S. And it is while I am struggling to articulate an appropriately sympathetic response and wondering why my friend was looking so chuffed about his progenitor's criminality, that I realise he must mean 'Yale,' as in the university, not jail, as in Alcatraz.

There is also the time that I go to a pharmacy in Madrid to look for some cream to moisturise my dry skin. The pharmacist peers at me and asks if I've 'heard of hell?!' For a moment I think she expects me, an obvious heathen, to fall down on my knees and accept Christ into my heart before it dawns that she is only offering an emollient gel.

In the aftermath of my mastectomy, I visit a physiotherapist; my shoulder is giving me trouble. But I begin the session by explaining that I have a problem with my husband, 'hombre,' when I mean, shoulder, 'hombro'.

Luckily, it is in the mistakes that you learn to laugh at yourself. Travel, when done well, decentres subjectivity. And travelling in new languages only amplifies this displacement of the ego, with a serving of giggles on the side.

4

PEDAGOGY

Some people believe in God. I believe in the Internet.

Ishaan at four years old

It is 2014. I am thirty-nine years old and clapping enthusiastically as my younger son walks onto the stage to receive a certificate from his school principal. Nico is being feted for having been 'caught being good'. Every Friday, the international school he attends in Jakarta awards this title at the morning assembly, to a child whom a teacher has spotted being particularly helpful or kind. Parents are invited to watch, and the whole auditorium is suffused with sweetness. Nico is puffy-cheeked with happiness (and a smidgeon of entitledness, an inner voice interjects).

What is this planet I have travelled to? So very distant from my school auditorium in New Delhi, where our morning assemblies involved watching the principal lean his body weight into the cracking slaps that he landed on the cheeks of children caught being bad. There were usually four or five boys—girls were exempt—on the daily slapping menu. They had been bad in a variety of enterprising ways. Someone might have let off a firecracker in the toilets. Someone else, caught smoking in a corner off the basketball court. Another's uniform might not have been up to scratch.

Regardless of the infraction, the correct consequence, according to our principal, Mr B, was a resounding slap. Dressed in a sparkling white polyester safari suit, the half-sleeved top of which spread tightly over his ample belly, the principal was a man with a straightforward and consistent sense of duty. He existed to catch and punish the errant among his flock.

Morning assemblies were conducted according to an unvarying formula. The students sat on the floor in lines arranged according to their year groups and sections. The principal loomed above on a stage, standing behind a podium. To kick things off, the whole school body engaged in some desultory singing: a mix of nation-praising and devotional songs. This was followed by two children from the 'house' that was 'on duty' that month, marching up to the podium. The first would read out a summary of the news, carefully copied out from the headlines of the day's newspapers. The second would then give a talk on a suitably ingratiating topic, like the 'Need for discipline in young people's lives'.

And finally, it was the moment that Mr B had seemingly been employed for. The Slapping. A line of wayward lads would be led up to stand beside him. As they ambled along, some looked shame-faced and red-eyed. Others stared out at the gathered student body defiantly, the half-smile of the martyr upon their lips. The principal's voice would reach thunderous levels of indignation as he called out each miscreant's offense, followed by the hard thwack of a smack. Sometimes, the white imprint of his hand stayed a while on the cheek of the child, all the blood squeezed out from the surface area of contact.

This ritual humiliation hardly caused a stir among the audience. Most of us were so acclimatised to The Slapping that we paid only minimal attention, preferring to play finger football with the large black ants that crawled about between us on the floor.

'Are you wanting me to be sending you to Mr B?' our middle-school geography teacher, Mrs U, who is as enthusiastic about gerunds as Mr B is about slapping, asks me. Its 1988. I am thirteen years old and instead of paying attention to the diagram of atmospheric layers in the textbook open in front of me, I've been whispering to my best friend about a cassette that my brother has managed to procure, with pop songs recorded off a US radio station.

The evening before, I'd spent hours playing and rewinding the songs on my tape recorder, trying to discern the lyrics and write them down in my beloved Snoopy-jacketed notebook. My set of friends were all heavily into the soundtrack of the film, *Flashdance*. A personal favourite, is a song called 'Fruit Juice Tonight'. It would take me many years to discover that it is in fact titled, 'Seduce Me Tonight'.

Unable to explain any of this to my geography teacher, I cast my eyes down in what I hope is a contrite look. Mrs U, who is prone to what I now know to be hot flashes, begins to sweat at the exertion of threatening me and deflates onto the desk. She dabs at her forehead weakly with the handkerchief she'd been clutching in her left fist. The right one holds chalk. 'Please, can someone be opening the window to let the climate in?' she gasps.

I attend what, in India, is called an English-medium school. It is a private school where the primary medium of instruction is in English. As Mrs U's argot exemplifies, this includes all manner of Englishes. It is an elite school, admission to which is prized. Classes are enormous. We are usually forty students in each section and there are six or seven sections that comprise each year group. The pedagogical philosophy stresses constant examinations, copious by-rote memorisation and regurgitation of facts.

And yet, between the slapping and exams, there is a wild freedom to the place which will give future descriptions of it a fictional feel. My children will come to treat my schoolgirl yarns as fairy tales—horrifying and fascinating. They will ask to hear them at bedtime, tickled by the idea of their mother in the role of a powerless child at the mercy of capricious adults. In place of wolves in grandmothers' clothes, evil witches and fairy godmothers, my stories feature teachers.

There is Mr P, the deranged maths instructor who throws thumbscrew compasses used for drawing circles in geometry at day-dreaming students. His precision is legendry. The compasses invariably land on students' desks, rather than their bodies.

The chemistry teacher, Mrs K, is very sexy. Her bare midriff, exposed by the chiffon sarees she favours, heaves suggestively as she discusses the attraction that variously charged atoms feel for each other. 'When one atom is positively *charged*,' she gasps huskily, 'it *bonds* (suggestive pause-titters from the back of the classroom) with a negatively *charged* one.'

There is a drunken high-school drama teacher whose hair bun gradually loosens as the morning wears on, in proportion to the slurring of her tongue. And an embittered biology pedagogue, who spends much lesson time lecturing us about how people like our parents don't pay taxes and ruin the nation.

A political science instructor begins all lessons with the rhetorical flourish: 'Are you a constellation of idiots or a galaxy of fools?' He bears a remarkable resemblance to Keshto Mukherjee, a popular comedian who is often typecast as a drunk in the movies. But physical resemblance aside, the political scientist gives no indication of imbibing anything stronger than water, unlike the drama teacher whose hip flask stays closer to her body than the wandering pallus of her sarees.

There is also Mr V, an English teacher, who takes a keen interest in me because of an essay I wrote that included a sentence along the lines of, 'I wish I were a scientist who might cure cancer.' He spent almost an entire class waxing eloquent on my use of the subjunctive mood, elated like a parched wanderer in a desert of 'was's, chancing upon the grammatical oasis of 'were'.

As students, we have scant expectations of our teachers regarding their domain expertise, pedagogical competence or even sobriety. School and the 'sirs' and 'ma'ams' who are its furniture, mirror the real, messed up, adult world outside the walls. There is very little playing nice and a lot of fending for oneself.

Where are our parents in this madding mix? Mine are divorced. My mother, whom I live with, works days as a sales executive at a five-star hotel. A few evenings every week she heads to the state-owned television station studios where she presents the 9 p.m. news in English. My mother is a celebrity, a nationally recognised face. But I think of her as a tiger mom, decades before the phrase enters the global lexicon. She is fiercely protective. She snuggles. But she also swats—Mr B is not the only slapper in the lives of children. And when she growls, it is terrifying.

Once, in primary school, I play truant from PE and make off for the playground instead. When found out, I am made to crawl around the sports field as punishment. My knees are scratched up by the end of the ordeal, but I am mostly relieved that the teacher doesn't send home a note for my mother. Then I would be in real trouble.

Writing about my school years in this manner feels somewhat disingenuous. On paper, it is terribly dark—this legacy of corporal punishment (British education's bequest to Indian schools), blended with parental neglect and garnished with a pinch of the general unpredictability of adults. But in experiential terms it was mostly fun, at least outside of the classroom.

Thirty years on, my school memories are sun-drenched, animated with the giggles of girlfriends as we failed to harmonise to Wilson Philips songs, or snuck a smoke in the toilets. The smell of bun samosas and instant noodles scents these snapshots. There were inter-school debate competitions and an annual dance drama performance that necessitated staying back for rehearsals, long past official hours. In my second year of high school, the drunk drama teacher directed a group of us with dishevelled brilliance in a version of Agatha Christie's *Witness for the Prosecution*.

Time lingered when I was that age. Free of past and future, it was a being wholly of the present. The dense, suffused quality of the hours we spent in school, allowed us to develop an almost romantic relationship with the building. Its red brick engendered a fierce loyalty; the sprawling lawns, deep pride. We would sit under the maternal shade of an old banyan tree and declare to each other that no matter how old we became, how far we travelled, *this* place, *this* time, *this* school would always be special.

I was part of a quartet of 'best friends'. We had no Instagram or private telephone access. School was our social life. It enabled our passion for each other, for relationships of choice not birth, for defining who we were by the things we looked down upon as uncool. One afternoon, when we were on the cusp of graduating high school, we swore to return to the same spot ten years later, when we were twenty-seven years old—so old, the imagination struggled to conceive of it. We really believed, each one of us, that we would.

In the event, none of us did. I was living in China by then. The temper of female friendships cooled once husbands and babies made their hot, demanding, appearances. Our school became a place we looked back on with bemusement. Were we really those people?

In Jakarta, Nico's assembly is over, and he is bounding up to me clutching his 'caught being good' certificate, awarded for his having been 'caught,' 'demonstrating empathy and inclusivity on the playground,' earlier that week. He takes me by the hand

and pulls me towards his classroom, where parents are invited monthly to look at the 'art' displays of their children.

Nico is in preschool 4, a year shy of grade 1. Classes have recently been focused on encouraging the five-year-olds to recognise their emotional state by associating them with colours. Red is angry, blue is calm, yellow is tired and so on. The paintings on display are pictorial representations of each child's preferred strategy of returning themselves to a 'blue' state, when agitated.

A little girl has drawn a stick figure eating a fish. 'When I'm sad, I like to eat salmon to feel happy again,' the teacher has printed out carefully below the masterwork.

Of all the travels I have been on by this point, none has matched the distance that pedagogy has journeyed from my childhood in New Delhi, to this international school in Jakarta.

On Mr B, the erstwhile principal's birthday, my social media feeds are always awash with former students waxing nostalgically on about being slapped by him. 'What a guy! What slaps! He taught me the meaning of respect,' read one homage a couple of years ago. To my boys' ears the idea of conflating 'the good old days' with public beatings is confounding. It is somewhat confounding to me as well, given that I have travelled through the decades to this other generation. How did I survive my school years with no notion that they were something to be survived? How did I feel so much nostalgia for what is intolerable from my present perspective.

The answer lies in the comfort with normative differences that travel engenders. Your idea of 'normal' is challenged when you move to somewhere with different rules to those that you have so far known.

For a Swede, shopping at an Ikea is probably experienced as the height of banality. But in the Beijing of the early 2000s, when I lived there, going to Ikea had been a family event, better than a visit to the zoo. Pandas were certainly cute, but in Ikea you could test the beds on sale by taking long naps on them. On

Sunday afternoons, the display beds were occupied by snorers whose snorts and whistles jostled for aural attention with the live band that played at the shop restaurant. I enjoyed watching grannies with Chairman Mao coiffures chowing down on exotic foods like Swedish meatballs at that restaurant, almost as much as watching Europeans in India exploding in excitement at the sight of 'water buffalos' on the streets.

A foreign name for the familiar changes the way you see it. Growing up, the sight of a *bhains* with its lumpy body and frumpy expression, wallowing in sludge, was so commonplace that the day's weather merited more attention. But when a visiting family friend from England pointed her finger at one and named it 'water buffalo,' it was as if she had waved a wand and shape-shifted the part-of-the-furniture bhains into an exotic *objet d'intérêt*.

It is only by travelling, in the sense of leaving behind the familiar, that the category of 'normal' becomes subject to deconstruction. The most extraordinary sight from my travels in Europe in my late twenties, was that of dog owners picking up their canine ward's faeces for post-walk disposal. It was the equivalent of a European's amazement at cows with ribbons on their horns, weaving through New Delhi's traffic. The more I crossed borders, the more I realised that everywhere—the mining towns of Colorado, the rat restaurants of Guangdong, the burning ghats of Varanasi, the bullfighting rings of southern Spain, are equally strange in their quotidian norms.

We are so much a product of the time and place we live in. But the greater the variety of times and spaces we come to inhabit, the more our ability to feel comfortable with a range of norms grows. Be these the norms of India or Japan or Mandarin or Cancer or Gen Z.

That said, there is also a tendency in all travel to push back against this burgeoning acceptance of difference. There will inevitably be times when we hanker for the familiar—to return home, to the kingdom of the well, or to the safety of our mother tongue. Harking back to one's childhood as a golden era is as natural as a New Yorker in Dhaka, finding herself longing for a good hot dog. It is at least partly why Mr B's victims recall his beatings with such fondness.

Like most young people, I'd spent much of my early adulthood rolling my eyes at my parents for their antiquated ways. But now, in this new country of my children's youth, I catch myself repeating the most annoying Mama-Papa mantras, my tongue hijacked by biology. On my fifteenth birthday, my father had presented me with a cheap watch. 'I got my first wristwatch when I was at university,' he'd intoned dolorously, seeming almost reluctant while handing me the present. I'd been left in no doubt that he considered me to be overly indulged. Twenty years later, I'd sounded equally sorrowful when I gave Nico his first plastic, Mickey-Mouse-decorated wristwatch on his fifth birthday. 'Here you go, lucky boy. Mama only got her first watch at fifteen,' I'd said.

This stickiness of our formative environment—an adhesive that even decades of travel can't fully dissolve—is why it has been difficult to avoid imposing the norms of my upbringing on my children. Changing the yardsticks by which we judge is travel's greatest gift, but even gifted travellers struggle to accept it.

In the decades I spent living in Asia—India/China/Indonesia/Japan—I learned that what bound the continent together was not trade or religion as much as the Ambitious Mother—a creature of the crazed competition that is the product of enormous populations and limited opportunities. For this maternal feline, her progeny's success is untrammelled by misery or trauma. She has this way of taking over my better judgement.

It is 2013. I am thirty-eight years old and terrifying my five-year-old son. He is trembling at my raised voice, wilting under my angry eyes, and hurting from my too-hard grip on his arm.

It hasn't always been like this, but I've just read a book and also, there was this corridor conversation with a fellow mom that has left me rattled.

My first-born, Ishaan, has just started at a school founded by one of Indonesia's wealthiest Chinese families. We have chosen this school, despite its high fees, because it is bilingual, and we hope our boy will learn Mandarin at an age when it is easier to absorb languages. The founder's daughter, a moon-faced child, is Ishaan's classmate. A few days ago, I learnt that this girl begins her mornings an hour earlier than the rest of the cohort, with a private wushu lesson. She is training to compete in an international martial arts competition. I was told this by her mother, with whom I happened to be waiting outside the classroom for school to give out.

The mom went on to casually mention that she was also training her daughter to kowtow to her in traditional Chinese style. 'I think it instils respect. Don't you?' she asked mildly, leaving my head spinning in a million directions as I thought of Ishaan's epic sassiness. Just the other day, he had asked why I could watch TV every evening when he was only allowed to on the weekends. 'Because I'm your mother and I can do whatever I want,' I had declared sternly. 'Oh?' Ishaan had countered. 'Can you climb a tree with no branches? Or cut down a coconut?'

In fatal happenstance, a few days before my exchange with the martial artist's mom, I had also begun to read Amy Chua's, *Battle Hymn of the Tiger Mother*. By the time I was through the first few chapters, some dormant genetic strain of Asian mom roared into life inside me.

Amy Chua had ensured that her daughter was an accomplished pianist by the age of six, obediently practising scales for hours every day. Her children were 'polite, interesting, helpful and well-spoken'. They did not go on playdates because they spent their 'free' time perfecting various intricate competencies. She explained that she hadn't let tears or tantrums deter her, because children always oppose learning a difficult new skill at the beginning, when they are not very good at it. Chua pointed out that this was where 'western' parents tend to give up. But by persisting even in the face of vehement opposition from the child, 'Asian' parents apparently create a virtuous circle wherein eventually a child begins to excel at the task at hand, and therefore, to enjoy it.

I was mortified. I'd been a terrible mother to Ishaan: lax and laissez-faire. While his wushu master classmate was already adept at calligraphy, Ishaan's writings were scarcely more than squiggles. Amy Chua had kept her daughters up until midnight perfecting their Chinese characters, but I heaped Ishaan with praise if he managed to distinguish his 'b' from a 'd'. The first time my son put his head underwater at swimming class I had leapt up and down clapping in encouragement and later bought him a milkshake in reward. Amy Chua would have refused to feed him at all until he had mastered the butterfly stroke.

When I looked at it with Tiger-eyes, it became clear that Ishaan was basically useless. He often coloured outside the margins in drawing class. By the time he managed to do up the buttons of his shirt, Amy Chua's daughter would have performed a dazzling Mozart concerto. I diagnosed the problem as lying within me. I had been craven in not insisting on perfection. I had let my son down by doing up his buttons for him when he was late for school, instead of waking up half an hour earlier to make sure he had enough time to redo the buttons again, and again, if necessary. I became determined to find my stripes.

For the next month, I sat down with Ishaan at a desk for hours after school, forcing him to write perfect ABCs. When he failed, I told him to try again, repeating that I believed he could do it if he only tried harder. I kept calm. For the first hour, or so. But eventually, I would lose patience and start yelling.

Which brings us to this moment. 'Why can't you just write the damn "p"?' I bellow, gnashing my teeth at his incompetence. He droops, this child of mine, this glorious, unique child who has displayed rare self-confidence and character from his toddling days. Only a month ago, he had announced that while, 'Some people believe in God, I believe in the Internet.' I wrote out the quote to frame and place on a kitchen shelf.

On my study desk there was a notebook filled with Ishaan aphorisms, often hilarious, sometimes unbelievably poetic.

There was the time when he was around two years old. He'd been grumpy and had rudely asked a visiting guest to leave. When I'd reminded him to be polite, he'd turned to the guest once again and said, 'Can you leave, *please*?'

At three, he'd bounded over to me after listening to a Bob Marley CD and solemnly pronounced that his favourite song was *Gruffalo Soldier*.

A year later, he said, 'You look like the rain, Mama, all black and golden.'

And here he is, failing to write a single word with even-sized letters over the course of an entire afternoon. I grip his shoulder so hard he winces, but I do not let up. We will not get up until he produces results.

In the end, my Tiger mania dissipates. My childhood and that of my boys' are different places, and I've always railed against being an ugly expat.

'Why do birds fly?' Ishaan asks me one Saturday morning. 'Because they have wings,' I say. 'I have wings too,' he replies. I look up, interested. 'Really? I can't see them. Where are they?' 'Oh, they're just resting, folded in my belly,' he says, mischief dancing in his eyes.

And just like that, I feel my claws retract, my stripes turning to a kaleidoscope of polka dots. My son is an imaginative and confident young person whom I have, in effect, been undermining. He is not Amy Chua's child. He is not the kowtowing-enthusiasts' son. He is all mine; a rockstar who dances to his own tune. The following school year, we withdraw Ishaan from the bilingual Chinese school and send him to the one where his brother and he will on occasion be 'caught being good'.

It is 2023. I am forty-seven years old, an Indian parent in Spain, and those claws are once again itching in their sheaths. Can tigers hibernate, like bears, I wonder? Why is my inner feline awakening after its decade-long slumber?

There is something about schooling in Spain that feels wrong, in the way that binge-watching Netflix, or eating out all week does: too easy, too indulgent. Being well-adjusted, rather than successful, is the goal for children in this new place. But although I have travelled across the generation gap and adopted the ways of this new world, early norms are like chewing gum on the sole of a sneaker. Despite all my practised code-switching, or perhaps because of it, I am bouncing between embracing the football and bemoaning the math.

Ishaan is about to go into his first year of high school. This is a pivotal moment; the point where his choices will begin to have real implications for his future. Humble bragging about progeny is rife among my former schoolmates from Delhi. A composite Indian flex of the type that I'm regularly subjected to goes something like:

'I don't know what to do with Rahul. He came second in maths, just as he's gone into the ninth. I mean, it's time to get serious now. And already it's second. Soon, it will be third and who knows what then? But all he wants to do is play chess. He won the district championship last month. Wants to be Vishwanathan Anand. Good, good. But what about his maths? What university will he get into at this rate?'

I also get earfuls of the Spanish parent equivalent:

'I don't know what to do with Alejandro. He's out almost every night. With girls! Already. Can you believe it? That boy is just too popular for his own good. Anyway, the one thing I'm thankful for is that he seems to be getting enough sleep, so he's on time for football practice. It's so important for children to play sports, no?'

Two matters loom large in the preoccupations of the parents of Ishaan's Spanish classmates: sports and socialising. Does my son 'go out' with his friends, they ask me. Does he play a sport? If I can answer in the affirmative to these two questions, then the assumption is that all is right in my offspring's world.

I am yet to have anyone enquire about his grades—probably because the school doesn't give him any. Until high school, children here get colour-coded end-of-the-year reports which emphasise 'attitude to learning,' and 'progress,' as much as achievement. The 'results' are shades of green, blue or red. I find it difficult to remember what any of the colours really mean. There is no sense of knowing how well the children are doing compared to others in the class—the pedagogical philosophy only encourages self-competition. Being better than your own past best.

I am well-acquainted with the ways of international schools by now. And yet. But. Hmmm. A reedy voice pipes up inside my head and asks me which university will be impressed by facts like my son did better than the year before? Or that he always keeps his desk neat?

Perhaps, Spanish universities? The rules of higher education here, compared to India's, are like steak to daal. Most children at my boys' Madrid school will go to a decent enough college. The public university system accepts the majority of applicants, being geared towards a democratic middle, rather than an upper-crust elite. It is why young people can spend their adolescence playing football and learning enough, in the security of the knowledge that their future, while perhaps not spectacular, will be just fine.

They don't need to spend hours in after-school tuition, depleted and anxious, because they do not live in an economy of scarcity. In Asia, the pressure is enormous. A quiet space to study in is a luxury. For many children, their marks in one exam determine their whole future. It's a one-shot culture.

I am here, in this fancy continent-spanning life, because I scored that shot. Again, and again. To get here, I first needed to do well enough in my school-leaving exams to get into the top arts and sciences college in the country. I scored the highest marks in three subjects in the world's second most populous nation to do so. Slam dunk. This college had an acceptance rate of about 1.3 per cent. Harvard University's acceptance rate by comparison, is well over 3 per cent today, and was at 18 per cent in 1993, the year I went to college.

Next, I had to do well enough in my first degree to get accepted for a second one at Oxford University. Dunk. And then, I had to get one of a handful of full scholarships to be able to attend. I scored again. Staying this road led me out into the whole world, even with an Indian passport—the heaviest of millstones around any would-be traveller's neck; even with no financial support from my culturally-elite, but financially hamstrung single mom.

The point is not to detail my academic achievements, fulsome though they were, as much as to recall to myself why these achievements had felt so nerve-rackingly necessary. They'd had a life-or-death quality to them. Both before my final high school exams and before my Oxford University finals, I had what I now recognise as mini-nervous breakdowns. I lost my appetite and cried constantly, haunted by thoughts of failure. I believed that to miss any one of the shots I had to score to remain on *the* path would leave me tethered when I wanted to fly. Were these fears overwrought? Probably. But at the time, they'd felt as urgent as the breath in my lungs.

My boys, on the other hand, are multiple-shot children. They can't fall down too far; their safety nets are right below their feet. Their Spanish passports are talismanic protection from resource scarcity. The worst-case scenario is an unexceptional, but good-enough, European university, followed by unexceptional, but good enough, careers.

My children's education has been a re-education for me. I'm learning to unlearn the idea that stress is essential to studying and that every exam is a dog fight. For my boys, the pie is substantial enough to share during football break. I am working on accepting this as an unqualified virtue. Being a good traveller is hard work.

But although travel helps develop an ease with a plurality of norms, this does not, nor should it, translate into an equal appreciation of all. In my view, the Japanese intolerance of noise could do with some relaxing, just as the Indian tolerance of the same needs tightening. Indonesians smoke too much. And Spain is in the wrong time zone, by two hours, I reckon. Three in the afternoon, is in fact, 1 p.m., were its clocks in consonance with its longitude, which explains the off-kilter meal timings. In England, it is time to ban the sale of sinks with separated hot and cold water taps that only allow handwashers to be broiled or frozen. And in the United States, the tipping culture is in urgent need of reform.

In this 'World According to Pallavi', the landscape of my children's childhood would be less littered with screens and more with paper and pen.

It is June 2023. I am sitting cross-legged on the floor of the room in New Delhi that my mother's corpse had occupied less than two days earlier. The smell of her sarees—what my younger boy calls the 'India smell' still hangs heavy in the room. I eye the three large cardboard boxes in front of me. They are groaning with the weight of letters addressed to the person I was between the mid-1980s and late 1990s. I find it difficult to comprehend that these oceans of words had once been composed for me, penned by an astonishing array of people, from close friends to people whom I barely knew in the corporeal sense.

I unfold an ageing aerogramme, the paper crackles; it is fragile, like my cracking, brittle heart. I have been enfeebled by my mother's passing. The letters are the detritus of a time when she was the sun that I revolved around. Without her, I am spinning in the dark, my thoughts eddying with a speed that makes them difficult to grasp, difficult to breathe. But the words on the pages I sift through have a steadying effect. They halt the feeling of erasure.

I find a stack of letters from a young South African woman I once met in a bar in Köln while backpacking across Europe in my late teens. I had forgotten about the correspondence that this chance encounter had birthed, one that lasted for about four years. I read some of her vivid descriptions of her university life. There is also a letter telling me about the tragic death of her older brother (whom I'd also met at that bar) in a freak car crash in Johannesburg. It's the last one I can find from her.

I rediscover a twenty-five-page letter from a university friend in the UK, dated the 17 August 1999, Wolfson College.

'Tuesday-Guildhall Arts Centre-pigging out on dripping cakes, mocha and that adrenalin-rich Glos ambience that we both love so dearly-and outside its drizzling anomie, the nasty fabrics of middle-aged women are being drenched, the seagulls have fled to sea, and me? And you? You could be a thousand miles away, I could be further—the mood it is listless and the heart is suspended, in the limbo between our lanky yesterdays and a tightfitting tomorrow. Don't ask me what I'm telling you about. I couldn't tell you-that's part of this morning's problem. That's what being here, right now, right here is like.'

I move on to another missive dated 1987, from an eleven-year-old school friend who had moved from India to Algeria with her diplomat father. At the end, she muses about the ethics of writing to me on paper, given the ecological impact of the destruction of trees.

There is one from my brother's former girlfriend (who was still current at the time of writing), from 1994. She is in Dubai with her parents:

'I've been here for a week now and have fallen into a comfortable schedule: wake up at noon, watch an inhouse movie till 2, work-out in the gym and swim till 3, eat lunch at 3:30, TV till 7:30 (Bold and Beautiful and Santa Barbara are on from 6-7:30 here), go out for dinner around 9, and then sleep by 1! My gym is not too rigorous

though, and so I'm indulging my natural propensity and putting on weight.

'Dubai is as racist as it is sexist – the white skins rule here, and all laws are bent for them. It's the 'native' from the subcontinent who has a tough time here. But I, of course, continue to go out in shorts and T-shirt, much to my father's discomfiture.'

There are pages and pages of minutiae. Friends describing life with the kind of self-reflection and care that feels alien, given the current lingua franca of smiley faces and thumbs-ups. The difference in the speed of communication shapes the content. Instant messaging is all about brevity and compression: lol, otw, rofl, lmao. Letter writing was about elucidation and patience. This knowledge of the passage of time between writing a letter and it being read is evident in how many of the letter-writers located themselves in space and time: I am sitting in the college common room; I am in the café we used to go to; I can hear the subway rumbling outside. Their handwriting is as much a part of how I think of them, as their eyes or braces or sense of fashion: sprawling, generous, fastidious, angular, galloping.

But quite soon, I can't bring myself to read any more. They recall too much of myself to me. It is such an unreliable thing, memory. So many of these epistles are packed with exquisite intimacies. And yet I can't recall having received them. Nor can I remember my part of the correspondence: the long, languorous letters I must have written, sitting in the family living room, or my university dorm, or whiling away the hours on a long train journey. The intervening decades have wiped so much of me off my own narrative arc. What a harsh editor memory is, selecting and compressing the months and years into scattered snapshots.

If a tree falls in a wood and no one hears it, did it really fall? If no one can remember what happened, did it happen? If you have letters to remember for you, then it did. So, I clutch them as if they are buoys. I run my hands across postcards and hastily scribbled notes. Many are torn or stained with coffee spills. They bear the traces of their journeys.

In this moment when my need for connection is greatest, the letters are presents from the universe, holding within them the efforts of the writers, my anticipation of receiving them, and the joyful patience of the entire process. My mother's presence is in them all.

Back in the territory of my children's world, I feel sad for their generation, for the texture of experience denied them by the loss of letters. I share my feelings with Ishaan. He rolls his eyes. 'You're so OG,' he mutters, 'old generation.' I have been labelled before. My husband once called me an 'unreconstructed Third Worldist'. The bursar of my Oxford college apparently referred to me as a 'bit of soot'. Europeans often assume I am British. It's an occupational hazard for a traveller to be labelled by the natives of the lands you visit. They don't necessarily mean any harm. It's just their way of getting a handle on your difference.

Often these labels can help you look at yourself through a new lens. It's something I try to do. So, I attempt to examine myself through the prism of being OG. It is true that I feel today's schools do a suboptimal job of teaching children to write by hand. The kind of spelling, punctuation and handwriting drills that comprised my primary school years are increasingly a thing of the past. The boys have been using laptops to turn in many of their assignments since primary school.

There are ways in which children today are more advanced pedagogically than I was at their age. Ishaan and Nico wield fearsome quantities of information on topics ranging from astrophysics to Roman mythology. In school, they are encouraged to read advanced texts and even to comprehend them. And yet, they spell poorly, their handwriting has the aesthetic qualities of a squashed arachnid, and their punctuation is as capricious as a toddler's dietary preferences.

As someone who keeps abreast of new ideas, despite being OG, I am aware that the Future of Work is important to keep in mind. Education needs to move along with the times. Given that our kids will rarely, if ever, need to handwrite, and will almost always have spelling and grammar software shaping their output, perhaps their time at school is better utilised towards gaining skills not so easily replaceable by artificial intelligence? Perhaps.

The reason for my hesitation isn't some anachronistic attachment to difficult spelling (I'm sold on a better use of time than learning how to spell diarrhoea). It's because in losing the art of writing, especially to each other, we lose the practice of introspection, the discipline of observation and the focus of mind that putting pen to paper inculcates. Letter writing is the antithesis of social media scrolling, coalescing instead of fracturing.

And so, although the handwriting drills of my school days might not have directly encouraged analytical thinking, they did prepare us to become letter writers. Am I being OG? Is that good or bad?

I put away the letters; it's getting late. That night, I begin to cry softly in bed. Nico, who has just turned twelve, gets in next to me and puts his still-tiny arms around my shoulders. 'You know what, Muma?' he says in a scientifically minded voice. 'When a star dies, it becomes a red giant and then a nebula and then a white dwarf. And then some white dwarves have a helium flash, and they are born as stars again.' The words hang between us. My future astrophysicist is sensitive enough not to belabour a point.

My children may not be letter writers, but their education has not been totally useless.

5

PASSPORTISM

I am a soul brother to everything that lives, to the giraffe and to the crocodile as much as to man.

Gustave Flaubert

It is January 2006. I am thirty years old and watching helplessly as my husband—the word still new on the tongue—is pushed out of the holding room at the Mexico City airport, where I have been shut in without explanation. An elderly Korean lady is the only other occupant. She doesn't make eye contact. There is nothing that gives away anything in this place. It is wholly featureless, without windows or texture. It is a non-place, just as I suddenly find myself a non-person. When I speak to ask what's going on, no one registers my voice. I have no right of refusal here. I must 'follow,' 'sit,' 'wait'. It doesn't matter how polite I am or how educated or how my moisturised skin indicates the use of expensive unguents. At this moment, as at many other times in the future, I am wholly defined by my passport, and it's a bad one: Indian.

I'm to attend the wedding of a Mexican friend I know from university in London. The bride and groom are taking us, the invitees, along with them on their honeymoon around the country. We will visit Oaxaca and Puebla. There will be pyramids and tacos and Frida. I've been beside myself with excitement, turning words like Popocatepetl and Quetzalcoatl around in my head, like 3-D objects. My husband has told me that the word 'tomato' comes from the Nahuatl *tomatl*.

But the excitement is of a tempered kind. Indian passport holders inevitably experience travel anticipation in a contaminated form. The purity of fantasy is alloyed with the toxin of visas. It is literally a dreadful excitement.

For my husband, to travel is a right, provided he can afford the plane fare; one that derives from his having been born in Alicante. For Delhi-born me, travel is a privilege to be earned by convincing visa officers that I am worthy, obedient, financially solvent. That I will return. That I won't attempt to get an illegal job as a dishwasher. I need to show bank account details and property papers, university degrees and police clearance certificates. I must always hold my breath until the page on my passport is stamped; until a bureaucrat somewhere is satisfied by my supplication.

When I'd received the invite for the wedding in Mexico, I'd immediately known I was in trouble. Applying for a Mexican visa with an Indian passport from China, where I lived, was going to be even less fun than filing convoluted tax returns in triplicate. Requesting a visa from inside India was difficult enough, but acquiring one from a third country always caused *haute* consternation. An Indian outside India was not in her proper place. She needed lots of extra scrutiny.

I made my way to the Mexican embassy in Beijing almost immediately after receiving the invite, for a trip that was still four months away. The lady at the consulate was alarmed. On my behalf. While fully sympathetic to my desire to attend the wedding, she revealed, sorrowfully, that the Mexican embassy's Beijing consulate could not process Indian visas. My passport would be taken from me and sent to Mexico City, where a background check, which would take a minimum of three months to complete, would determine whether or not I was travel-worthy.

The alternative, she said, was to return to Delhi and apply from the Mexican consulate there. This would expedite the decision to a matter of weeks rather than months. Since I did not have the money to buy a plane ticket to return to India solely to apply for a visa, nor the requisite time off from my job, there was little option but to entrust my passport to Quetzalcoatl and to wait. I waited for just over three months, after which I got a call from the consulate lady. 'Good news,' she said, audibly excited. 'Your visa is approved. Please come and collect your passport.'

This is why I am stunned. I had jumped as high as I'd been asked to. I had filled in the forms and been verified across continents. I was solvent. I'd been good. Now I realise that I was mostly just naïve. While waiting in the immigration line at the airport, I'd dared to not feel anxious. I had chattered with my husband about what we were going to do as soon as we'd collected our luggage. I'd forgotten how long the distance between passport control and the luggage carousel is for people like me. Being married to a white European was an amnesic.

My husband was ahead of me in the queue. The immigration official glanced at his visa-less Spanish passport for a nanosecond and gestured him through. I was next, and I approached with the confident smile of the correctly certified. The official did not smile back as he took a long, hard look at me and then began to slowly flip through my passport. There was such menace in the deliberation with which he turned each page. Back and forth, back and forth. Perhaps he couldn't spot the visa, given that my passport was crammed with them. I reached out to indicate the correct page, only to have him recoil, as if punched. My spluttering explanations were abruptly terminated as he hoisted himself out of his chair and asked for me to follow him. 'Why?' I said, bewildered. 'What's going on?' asked Julio. Our words were lost in the hot, close air.

My nerves are jangling, mind uncomprehending, as I wait in this cell. Why am I in what is effectively jail, instead of with my friends? I imagine them getting impatient at our lack of egress, and my anxiety mounts. Why can't I speak to my husband? Why will no one say anything? I am angry. And then I am just tired. It's been a monstrous trip from Beijing to Mexico City. I glance at the Korean lady. She has barely moved.

After about half an hour, or is it ten hours, the door to the room swings open. An airport official points at me. 'You can go,' she says. There is no further explanation of what has just gone down. I spot my husband hovering behind the lady. We clutch hands, hurry to the exit, and disgorge ourselves into the hubbub of the arrival hall.

There is a certain type of person, and I count myself among this demographic, who equates travel with virtue. We proselytise crossing borders as a way of breaking free of narrow domestic walls. We advise moving outside of our comfort zones as fodder for curiosity and empathy. We feel kinship with the cosmopolitanism of the ancient Greek philosopher, Democritus, who said: 'To a wise man, the whole earth is open, for the native land of the virtuous soul is the entire world.'

But amidst this conception of travel as self-improvement, the question of who gets to travel, and under what circumstances, is easily ignored. A young German male backpacker and an older, head-scarved, Iranian woman may travel on the same planet, but these might as well be in different solar systems. Race, religion, gender, class, and above all, nationality have determined the caste system of global travellers for the entirety of my life, a hierarchy that is only getting more ossified.

It is June 2025, and I am forty-nine years old. A few weeks earlier, the United States President, Donald Trump, ordered US embassies around the world to stop scheduling appointments for student visas, as the administration prepared to better vet the social media world of applicants. A thumbs up to the wrong thought, coupled with the wrong passport, and borders become straitjackets.

Yesterday, a new proclamation restricts, or wholesale denies entry to nineteen passports, including those of Afghanistan, Burma, Chad, the Republic of Congo, Equatorial Guinea, Burundi, Cuba, Laos, Sierra Leone, Togo, Turkmenistan, Venezuela, Eritrea, Haiti, Iran, Libya, Somalia, Sudan and Yemen. The visa bans are purportedly a response to a terror attack on 1 June , that injured eight people in the state of Colorado. The perpetrator of the attack is an Egyptian national who had overstayed his visa. Egypt is not on the list of countries with limited or total visa bans.[1]

Passportism has much of the caste system's ingrained randomness in its bigotry, with national security as fig leaf. First World–passport holders are hereditary brahmins, with the rest of the globe fitting into differing levels of hierarchy.

I am reading Shahnaz Habib's *Airplane Mode,* in which she recalls attending a travel documentary-related job talk whilst in graduate school in the United States.[2] The PowerPoint presentation began with a discussion of the vacation-related habits of peoples from different parts of the world. 'Europeans travel in August', 'cruises are for retired Americans,' etc. The final, punchline slide read: 'People from the Third World do not travel, they immigrate'.

Those who identify as sensitive travellers are often flashy virtue signallers. They volubly abhor racism, sexism, homophobia et al. Their cosmopolitan values are in opposition to these blinkered world views. But the most basic enabler of travel for global brahmins, the passport, is also the greatest impediment to free movement for the world's backward castes. And yet, passportism, or discrimination against Third World passports, somehow hides in plain view, as a perfectly valid form of bias, free of the moral repugnance that casteism and its ilk provoke.

Most passport brahmins remain blithely unaware of the humiliations inflicted on those less privileged. This ignorance is in the same vein as in which white people often declare there to be no racism because they have never experienced it. But unlike other forms of prejudice, passportism has an objective ranking. According to the Global Passport Index[3], a French passport allows one to travel to 135 countries without a visa. For an Afghan national, that number is seven.

Given how today, a French passport is the equivalent of a key to the world, it is ironic that the document has roots in the locking down of undesirable movement. In France, as in many parts of Europe, including Britain and Russia, passports were originally intended to limit the movement of peasants from the countryside to the cities.[4] Saddling peasants with the necessity of travel permits protected city dwellers from overcrowding and resource scarcity, allowing them their pleasant, rabble-free gentility.

In contemporary times, there is an equivalent in the Chinese *hukou*—an internal passport that polices the access of people from rural areas to urban spaces in China.[5] Despite its metaphorical association with access—think of phrases like 'a passport to a better life'—a passport is almost always as much about restriction, a hydra-headedness that remains embedded in contemporary passportism.

Another kind of travel document, one granting safe passage to the bearer in foreign lands, issued in the name of a royal or religious eminence has an even longer history. The earliest mention of one appears in the Old Testament of the Bible, wherein the prophet, Nehemiah is granted letters from the ancient Persian King Artaxerxes, requesting the governors of the lands beyond the Euphrates to grant him safe passage to Judah (modern-day Israel/Palestine).

In Britain, the first reference to a 'safe conduct' document dates to a 1414 Act of Parliament, during the reign of Henry V. Almost 200 years later, in 1599, Shakespeare made a lyrical reference to this early passport in his play about the same monarch. On St Crispin's Day, on the eve of the Battle of Agincourt, the bard has Henry V urge his men to fight against the larger French forces.

'That he which hath no stomach to this fight, / Let him depart; his passport shall be made,' said the fictional Henry V.

If visas had existed then, caveats would have been needed. 'Let him depart; his passport shall be made, although that gent shall needeth to waiteth f'r a visa appointment and yond might seeth that gent well into fusty age. Bett'r to just square the French.'

Henry himself, like all successive monarchs, was not subject to the need for a passport to travel, the argument being that passports are issued to British nationals in the name of the ruler. Even today, King Charles remains *sans*-passport, the ultimate by-birth brahmin.

In fact, for much of the nineteenth century, travel brahmins—high-born men from white nations—could swan about the world without passports and with servants, if their bearing was sufficiently haughty to ensure that no questions were asked. If you looked like you were born to mobility, you could usually enjoy it.

Passports, as we recognise them today, made an appearance only about a century ago, rising from the ashes of the First World War. The Great War accentuated the nation-ness of nations. Questions of who properly belonged inside what boundaries became exigent, ostensibly on grounds of national security. In 1920, the League of Nations suggested a worldwide passport standard.[6] Four years later, the United States passed the Immigration Act of 1924 to limit the influx of immigrants to the right kind. And how did one determine who was right and who wrong? By identifying their country of origin via their passports.[7]

There are multiple ways to discriminate based on colour: skin yes, but also travel documents.

The cleverness of the passport as a standard for sorting humans, lies in its purported objectivity. Imagine someone who is a staunch believer in Enlightenment values and, as a corollary, is appalled by the caste system. It would be rather awkward for this someone to justify the restriction of the mobility of another, purely based on the colour of their skin or religion. The passport, however, is the hypocrite's ally.

(What do you notice about the colour and religion of most of the countries on this list: Afghanistan, Burma, Chad, the Republic of Congo, Equatorial Guinea, Burundi, Cuba, Laos, Sierra Leone, Togo, Turkmenistan, Venezuela, Eritrea, Haiti, Iran, Libya, Somalia, Sudan and Yemen.)

In *Airplane Mode*, Habib details the colonial roots of current passportism. It was important for the British Empire to be able to move indentured labourers between various territories, depending on the need for either labour, or cannon fodder. Indians were sent off to Fiji, to Malaysia, to the Caribbean, to grow sugarcane and rubber. Regiments of the Indian army fought in Flanders Fields, Egypt and across the Far East.

But, when colonised people began to autonomously express a desire to travel to other parts of the empire for reasons that had nothing to do with back-breaking agricultural labour or dying for the king, the colonial administration became less keen on free movement.

The migration of some 2,000, brown-skinned Sikh men to Canada in 1905, for example, caused great consternation in the white dominion. The governor general of Canada demanded their deportation, claiming disingenuously that the climate would not suit the would-be immigrants.

Now, the British were publicly committed to the idea that Empire was a force of good for the natives, making it discomfiting to tell the truth—that the darkies needed to stay put. Convoluted policies ensued. In Canada, a 1908 law was devised that permitted entry to only those travellers who arrived via direct passage from their country of origins. No layovers were permitted. Conveniently, there were no shipping companies that offered a non-stop voyage between India and Canada.

A few years on however, enterprising Indians began to board ships from Hong Kong and Shanghai, meeting the continuous journey requirement. It was in the passport that a final solution to the conundrum of all people being equal, but some more than others, was found. A British Indian passport was issued to a limited number of Indians—entitling a few to free admission across the Empire, while denying movement to the vast majority of the passportless.

It is June 1994. I am eighteen years old, and smoking with imagined aplomb, aboard a rickety Uzbekistan Airline plane. My eyes sting, my throat is parched, but I am aflame with freedom and nervous excitement. A sense that I am about to begin Life hops in my stomach—and smoking without the need to hide from the parental panopticon is symbolic of this liberty; an autonomy in consonance with flight. I am aloft in a myriad ways.

The plane is taking me from New Delhi, where I have recently started university, to Oxford, where my older brother is just wrapping up his studies. My route, via Tashkent, might be unorthodox, but it is cheap. Uzbekistan airlines is barely two years old at this point, having been established in early 1992, following the dissolution of the Soviet Union. The planes themselves are a lot older than the airline, but I am young—and the age of planes does not register, only the price of tickets.

I have been funded, somewhat meagrely, by my father to join my brother on a month-long trip interrailing across Europe. I have a rail ticket that allows me unlimited journeys on a network of trains that crisscross the continent, £600 to cover all expenses, an international youth hostel card, and a rucksack. My brother, five years my senior, has been entrusted to act as my chaperone and guide. He has planned for us to visit France, Germany, Austria and Italy. I've had no say in the itinerary or much else, but I have determined to be as unobtrusive as possible. The fear that I will wake up to realise that it's all been a fevered dream, is real. I am treading softly, unbelieving of my luck.

The name of each country is so exciting that my nerves do the quick step as I imagine walking their streets, being *in* places sprung from the pages of the books that had, for the most part, been my portals to travel until then.

I spend several hours over a couple of months outside various embassies in Delhi, applying for visas. We are in a pre-Schengen, pre-visa outsourcing world. I meet with consulate officials, many of whom are kind, and excited for me, stirred out of their boredom by my unusual profile. I am an exotic case: not a would-be immigrant, not a student, not part of a family of holiday makers, not a man, not embarking on an arranged marriage with a European passport holder.

I am a female adolescent, about to perform the kind of modernity they approve of. I fit the travel as 'finishing school' paradigm, which has a hoary history in Europe. I wish to travel to glean experiences that are outside of any institutional curriculum, mayhap to kiss a stranger. The consular officers 'get' the idea of a young person seeking the kind of self-realisation that occurs while sipping a glass of wine on an Italian piazza. The visa officials smile and press stamps into my passport with generous attention. They wish me 'bon voyage'.

I wouldn't be surprised if they discuss my application over family dinners. It's one they're unlikely to have come across often, in India—a place where after-school maths tuition is the standard version of 'finishing school'. Where the idea of travelling to foreign countries often makes people anxious about what they will eat. 'Foreign' is not a place for enjoyment when you are unsure whether your accent will be understood. When you fear causing offence with your saree-clad bodies or your too slow way of walking. For many Indian parents sending their eighteen-year-old daughter off to loiter across Europe would be an almost criminal act of irresponsibility.

Mine are unicorns. Their permissiveness and my wanton desire for movement betray my deracination, a state that my English-speaking tongue already hides in plain sight. I am sailing forth on gossamer wings of cultural confidence, having read the right books, developed the 'right' kind of secular outlook, and clad in jeans and a tee.

There is always a degree of smoke and mirrors when it comes to our identity, but more so with Macaulay's descendants, like me. I haven't questioned who I 'am' much, yet. I need to travel to begin that excavation.

And so, before I buy my Uzbekistan airlines ticket to the world outside, I finger through my passport with the five glorious stamps it is now decorated with. I feel like the infant Lord Krishna who contained the whole world within his mouth. My muggle identity is already evident in the mélange of allusions with which I make sense of my internal world.

Interrailing is the late twentieth century version of The Grand Tour—the cross-continental journey that was popular, between the seventeenth and nineteenth centuries, in aristocratic circles in Europe, as a way of 'finishing' a young man's education. These travels, which could last years, were intended to hone his social graces and broaden his cultural horizons. The route comprised the greatest hits of continental offerings: Paris, Basel, Geneva, Flanders, Vienna and, always, most importantly, the art-drenched cities of Italy.

By the mid-nineteenth century, wealthier members of Europe's middle classes also began to travel, climbing the social hierarchy by imitating the behaviour of the nobility. Later, as the middle class grew apace with the infrastructure for the railways, commercialised mass tourism was born and the travel guidebook emerged as its midwife.[8]

The most notable amongst these guides, were those by Karl Baedeker, who founded his Koblenz-based publishing house in 1827. These were the McDonalds of early European travel: making what could have been a confounding experience, standardised and accessible. First-time travellers were unburdened of choice or discernment. They could simply follow what the books told them to do.

The conventions of Baedeker guides have had remarkable staying power, their shadow looming over the bibles of 1990s travel, *The Lonely Planet* and *The Rough Guide*. Exploring the European continent by the time I am about to embark on my journey is a more democratic exercise than it was a century ago. Only black, brown, east-Asian (Japanese excepted) and indigenous peoples are noticeably absent on the circuit. The bio-persona of *The Rough Guide* that my brother has purchased to usher us along our way is a young, white, middle-class, backpacker, who wants to travel on the cheap. The question of 'cheaper than what,' remains uninterrogated.

By consuming the Rough Guide, I feel included in a demographic within which I am an imposter. The book addresses a me that is not really me. My priorities are misaligned with the intended reader. Ensuring I don't overstay my visa (each country has issued me a permit for precisely the number of days and dates I have told them I will visit) is a far bigger preoccupation than choosing the restaurant with the best view. And yet, I trill to the headings: sleeping, eating, entertainment, tours, sights, festivals, top ten. The guide is my Blakean grain of sand. I see in it the keys to the world.

In the decades since, nothing has quite measured up to the moment I emerge out of the Köln train station, into the open. I almost topple over backwards at the sight of the Dom, the city's high-gothic cathedral, in infinite upward spiral. The impact is physical. I am unable to look at it without feeling as if I will fall off something, even though I am standing on flat ground.

Poncho-clad Peruvian buskers are whistling on flutes. Young people in sleeveless vests mill about. A girl's long ponytail glints in the sun like spun gold, a well-mannered dog at attention by her side. The scent of a sausage stand, somewhere close, floats on the light breeze. Köln is the first stop on our European itinerary and my first, exotic experience of a public space as somewhere to linger rather than to elbow one's way out of. This new-found understanding only intensifies as the month wears on and we tick off the boxes on our circuit: Köln, Berlin, Munich, Leipzig, Dresden, Innsbruck, Vienna, Salzburg, Rome, Venice, Florence, Cannes, Toulouse.

We take a cruise down the Rhine and get off at the wrong stop to discover that we have missed the last train out to anywhere. There are no hotel rooms available. There is no script to follow. A stranger overhears us trying to explain our predicament at the tourist office in town and indicates for us to follow her. We are so young and trusting, and frankly out of options, that we obey. Communication is through sign language. The lady takes us to her home and gives us her spare room for the night. The next morning, she cooks us breakfast before dropping us off at the train station. An angel from Bingen.

In Munich, we eat sausages from an *imbiss* at Marienplatz. A little girl stares at me, her face all eyes. The girl's mother shoos her off and says, 'She has never seen anyone with your skin colour.'

Later, at the railway station we need information on which train to take for the Dachau concentration camp. But my brother and I are loathe to cause embarrassment. How would a German person feel to be asked the whereabouts of a concentration camp by two Indian tourists? Discomfited, we imagine. While we deliberate, a drunkard sprawled out on the floor next to us, snaps out of his stupor to snarl something ugly at us in German. We step backwards, startled. Almost immediately, a woman appears and shouts him down. She turns to us and apologises profusely. 'I am so sorry.' 'I am so sorry.' We have no idea what has gone down. I am a little uneasy, but mostly elated that things are happening to me.

On a train to Florence, we share a compartment with two university students from Texas. When we tell them we are from India, they look a little lost. Then one of them snaps her fingers, 'Oh right! The Budapest place?' On other trains, travellers with passports different from ours advise us to change our plans. 'Go to Croatia,' many say. It's unspoilt and so cheap. We nod politely and do not burden these interlocutors with a lesson in passportism.

The days slip by like beads on a rosary. Busking and free museums; drinking water out of the taps in bathrooms; city squares where young women laugh up at the sun and no one gives them a second look. I soak it up. In Italy, my brother is pickpocketed. Twice. On consecutive days. By the time we arrive at our last stop on the tour—Toulouse in France, he is a tad disgruntled. But I am without exhaustion. I want to move ceaselessly, to transgress, to shed. We visit a beach peopled by nudists. At first, the shock of naked breasts and penises is like a kick in the gut. But then I strip down to my underwear and wade into the water, feeling see-through with pleasure. Afterwards, we cycle back to our accommodation, the wind on my bare legs—I am clad in only a crumpled T-shirt over my wet bra and panty. I am ungovernable.

It is 1998, four years since my travels across Europe. I have recently returned home to New Delhi, having sat my finals at university in the UK earlier in the summer. But home no longer fits—the traveller's curse. The new lens of elsewhere tints everything, and it isn't rosy. I am twenty-two years old, an aspiring journalist. While completing an internship on the foreign desk of a leading national daily, I write a piece about my homecoming, which is published in the weekend section of the paper. The writing is gauche and excessive, although the sentiment, sincere. I am still uncooked, the blush of adolescence lingering on the cheek.

'**City Revisited**:

What strikes me first about this city of ours, Delhi, is the cloying atmosphere of repressed sexuality. Everywhere, women—as they hail autos, buy onions, queue for cinema tickets, stare fixedly at the floor. Not out of fascination for the bacteria on terra firma, but to avoid the shame of acknowledging the lascivious stares of all the men that Delhi roads seem to teem with. They lounge around in gaggles and appear to do little save emit a steady stream of 'O! Lailas,' 'very nice,' or 'sex-bomb!'

What strikes me second, is the almost universal acceptance of this kind of treatment of women by both sexes, including sometimes, myself. After a long day's work, I get too tired; it's pointless to be angry all the time. And worst of all 'eve-teasing' (as harassing women is euphemistically referred to in India) can become so routine that I forget there's anything to be angry about; that maybe it's perfectly acceptable for a productive citizen of this country to be unable to walk to the local market without being ogled at, and not uncommonly, touched.

I've seen young girls fall prey to passing cyclists. I've personally been physically harassed in a crowded bus and was too frightened, too shocked, to do anything save move away. And such violence—for these are violent acts, psychologically and often physically—has somehow permeated our social fabric. Indian culture and values, of which the world often gets a mouthful from legions of chest-thumping patriots, are deeply misogynist.

In my finite experience, there has been little evidence of the glorious respect for women that our Bharatiya Sanskriti (Indian cultural heritage) is ostensibly an apotheosis of. Why are long-suffering victims of male abuse glorified, while sexually forward women censored or caricatured as prostitutes? Indian culture has become diseased with an ulcerous morality. It is the wont of culture and morality to be fluid. Yet too many seem determined to freeze ours in an ontological trap.

This puzzles me: the extent to which we are defensive, quick to reject any influence from across the seas as cultural imperialism—destructive or obscene. This seems to include everything from 'dirty' MTV videos, to wearing a seat belt.

The deepest misconception appears to lie in the idea that censorship is the panacea to all ills. I would prefer a culture where everyone indulges in gluttonous phone sex, if riding a bus ceased to be a traumatic experience.

Dilli: the seat of the mighty Mughals, the jewel in the crown of the erstwhile British empire, the subject of ecstatic poets and exquisite prose—remains a cruel city.

And yet, I love it. Mourn for it. When away, long for it. As a student in Oxford, I extolled its virtues: the grandeur of the Red Fort, the leafiness of Lodhi Gardens, the charm of shopping at Janpath and the excitement of Rajpath lit up at night. Even the white tiger at the Delhi Zoo, morphed in my tellings from pale yellow and rather limp, to a gigantic, sparkling beast as I enthralled foreign friends with tales that were only a little tall.

I was evidently persuasive, for half a dozen enraptured students had rushed for their Lonely Planet guides and cheap return fares before I could shout, 'Don't!'

For I'd forgotten in my enthusiasm to mention to Asthmatic American what breathing Delhi air did to healthy lungs. Buxom Brit had no idea that in Delhi breasts tended to be treated like communal property by passersby. Black Botswanian was vastly unprepared for the sniggers and racist slurs she was likely to encounter. It was shaming for me that I'd allowed myself to be indoctrinated by the purple prose of patriotism, lulled into a romantic Mark Tully-esque view of Dilli-O-Dilli.

Is it hopeless then? Yes, if we continue to be divided between the wearily cynical and smugly parochial. Delhi is no paradise, but neither is change impossible. Maybe if we all started being a little less 'adjusting,' and getting a little angrier, I could stop writing articles like this one and indulge instead in euphoric eulogies of this City of Djinns, like I always wanted to when I grew up.'

The piece attracts haute indignation. For the next few days, the newspaper's 'Letters to the Editor' section exclusively carries reader responses to it, under the heading, 'Ire for Aiyar'.

'It seems Ms Pallavi Aiyar is highly prejudiced. I have also returned to India after six years studying and working in the US, but I still have immense regard for my country. It is pathetic that in the space of two years India has become intolerable for her. May I remind her, that in spite of everything, this is the country of her birth, her parents and is the same as it was 2 years ago.'

'I would like to remind Ms. Aiyar of John F Kennedy's famous plea to his countrymen: Ask not what your country has done for you, but what you have done for your country.' Her piece smacks of ignorance and arrogance. Granted, India is not the best place to live in, so let us do our bit first and then criticize.'

'I would advise Ms. Aiyar to do the right thing. Go back to green England. You have your own life. Time wasted brooding over lost chances will carry hurtful memories when you are grey and old. All your life you will continue to blame everyone and turn cantankerous.'

'Those people, like Ms. Aiyar, are the special type of our countrymen who should be better known as UBI (Unfortunately

Born in India). They never miss a chance to show their pseudo-intellectualism and fabricated ill-will by downgrading Indian culture and Indianism. In my opinion, we Indians are really unfortunate that we are bound to address Ms Pallavi Aiyar, an Indian.'

After three days, the subject is closed for discussion.

At first, I am bewildered. And hurt. Being trolled on twitter, (compared to which these letters are the height of courteous subtlety) is an experience of the future. But once the initial shock of having generated such ire passes, I am contemptuous. The replies, I tell myself, betray an unreflexive patriotism, in direct contraposition to my cosmopolitanism. I have touched a nerve, and thin skin, I think, equals thick insecurities. Narrow-minded, petty, bigoted, ungrammatical, I fume.

I decide that the irate responses to my 'common sense' observations are proof of why one has to travel in order to become clear-eyed about 'home'. Travel makes the invisible quotidian, visible. In a commencement speech at Kenyon College, a decade down the line, David Foster Wallace would open with this story: 'There are these two young fish swimming along and they happen to meet an older fish swimming the other way, who nods at them and says 'Morning, boys. How's the water?' And the two young fish swim on for a bit, and then eventually one of them looks over at the other and goes, 'What the hell is water?'

Travelling is the process of recognising the water. What you do with that recognition might be outside of travel's pedagogic role, but the mutating of implicit norms into explicit ones, is an important step towards a more critical understanding of self.

All of this is true. But what I am too young and full of righteous pride at this moment to have, is empathy. To try and understand why so many people have been annoyed by my words. I am unable, as yet, to see that the superiority of perspective I have accrued to myself by virtue of having travelled, is arrogant and to many, irritating. I cannot put myself in the shoes of the reader to whom my writing feels judgmental and juvenile: a deracinated temper tantrum.

The traveller's sense of broadened horizons can be a taunt to those who have lacked the same opportunities. The material and cultural capital that enabled me to travel outside of India is a privilege, magnified by a deeply unequal society. Choosing cosmopolitanism over patriotism is not always, or simply, a matter of making the more virtuous choice. It is at least as much about being lucky. About birth. About caste. About language. About passports.

That said, I stand by everything my twenty-three-year-old self wrote in that first published piece.

It is 2022. I am forty-six years old and close to screaming. Tick-tock, tick-tock, the minutes go excruciatingly by as I hold a phone to my ear and there is only muzak on the other end. I am due to attend a literature festival at the British Library in London, in three days' time. Like a good girl, I'd applied for a UK visa seven weeks in advance of my travel dates. Being a long-time journeyer in the world of visa applications, I'd imagined this to have been plenty of time. Ha, ha! That, dear reader, is the hollow laughter of bitter hindsight.

The application procedure had been akin to the labours of Hercules, except tougher than slaying a mere Hydra. The time when you applied at a counter manned by a human being with discretionary power, as had been the case back in my Euro-railing days, was a bygone era. Most embassies around the world now outsource the collection of applications to private companies, making for a process about as transparent as the workings of the standing committee of the Politburo of the Chinese Communist Party.

The first step was to fill out some eighteen pages worth of an online form that asked me to list every country I had travelled to in the last ten years, with dates of entry and exit. Given that pre-

Covid I'd spent a lot of time in the air, this was a bit like asking for an annotated Odyssey. There was also the Iliad of insulting, intrusive questions about my salary and bank balance, and the Mahabharata of supporting documents required to back all this up.

A ten-year visa would cost me almost 1,000 euros, a sum I could not spare. I decided therefore, to apply for the cheapest, six-month-long entry permit, figuring it would also be the quickest to get approved. On arrival at the visa collection centre in Madrid, I was greeted by a bouquet of signs asking for more money.

> Access our Premium Lounge for £ xxx
> Skip the queue for £ xxx
> Help available to upload your documents for £ xxx

It was like a Tesco supermarket, albeit one that professed total ignorance about its wares. Emphatic notices abounded, stating that the application collection centre was only a commercial partner of the UK government, with no access to information about the status of applications, so don't inquire.

My biometrics were taken, and then, to my consternation, so was my passport. I asked how long they'd keep it for. I got a shrug in response. The Kafkaesque realm of UK visas is one where the traveller is parched for information. The British embassy in Madrid claimed they had nothing to do with visas. The visa collection centre to which the embassy had outsourced these procedures, said they had nothing to do with decisions. I was pointed to a website which appeared to have been designed by someone with the intuitive capacity of a block of wood.

After waiting fifteen days with no response, I finally tracked down an email I could write to. I had to pay for a response that would take a week in arriving. I paid. And waited. When it finally came, the response said that there was no information available about my application.

Which is why I am now on the phone, trying to speak to a human being. I am supposed to be in London three days later. I have an air ticket and hotel room, but neither a passport nor a visa. Upon dialling the number, I'd been prompted to provide credit card details, which I did. And so, tick-tock, I am now waiting, tick-tock. Finally, maybe five minutes—and who knows how many pounds—later, there is a homo sapien on the other end. She says she is unable to provide any details on the status of my application. She says that she understands my frustration and apologises for the inconvenience.

I had studied for two university degrees in the United Kingdom. My photo is up on the British Library website selling tickets for an event it now seems I won't be at. But passportism is blind to accomplishments.

In 1999, a year after winning the Nobel Prize in Economics, Amartya Sen and his Indian passport were detained at the Zūrich airport, where he'd landed on his way to speak at the World Economic Forum in Davos. In a *New York Times* interview, Sen recalled how the airport police were 'very sceptical about my financial means'. The Nobel laureate, who was at the time master of Trinity College in Cambridge and a Harvard professor, produced his US green card, credit cards and a letter from the Swiss Embassy in London promising him a visa at the airport, but to little avail. Immigration officials demanded a bank statement to prove that he was solvent. He was held for more than an hour before finally being let in.

As for me, various worthies in both Spain and New Delhi stage last-minute interventions with diplomatic officials, so that my visa miraculously appears the day before I need to travel. Later, I write thank-you emails to these officials for the 'courtesy' extended to me.

I have been in a relationship with a passport brahmin, my husband, for almost a quarter of a century at the time of writing.

Marriage is the easiest way to upgrade your passport. And yet, I have hung on to my Indian travel document. My relationship to it is akin to having a bad boyfriend, based on an impractical—my friends tell me, wrongheaded—affection. It's about romantic notions rather than bald facts. It pays no heed to the tortured realities of visa applications and routine humiliations at the hands of immigration officials in a bad mood. It erects barriers—both corporeal and metaphorical—between me, and my husband and children, who are all Spanish citizens.

And yet, I have hung on to it, mulishly, not always able to explain why. When I try and examine the reasons, they are confused. There is love and loyalty mixed in, but at the heart of the decision, lies guilt. I am troubled by the notion that were I to trade up for mere convenience, I would be selling out. Amassing greater ease to a life that has already been given more than its fair share by the roll of the cosmic dice feels gluttonous.

Indian independence, its existence as a free country, was so hard fought for. Its future is far from secure. I have a personal and emotional investment in its ongoing struggles. My passport, I have convinced myself for years, is proof that I have skin in that game. But what is really at the root of my reluctance to swap passports is the unarticulated need to atone for my privilege as a high caste, English-speaking, culturally advantaged Indian. It's the guilt from the obscenity of belonging to India's one per cent. The one thing that puts me on an equal footing with every other Indian, regardless of caste or creed, is my passport. If I suffer from trudging about the land of visas, it's a suffering I share with my compatriots.

The extent of this 'sharing' is overstated, of course. Journeying in visa country is easier for people like me who know worthies able to intervene on their behalf at a pinch. Who have laptops and electricity that enable them to fill out online forms, and the economic means to be able to pay for visas. Nonetheless, an Indian passport grounds me. It reminds me, as the writer Tabish Khair has put it, of 'how marginal I am in the global heart of whiteness ... of what I share with the Nepalis, Algerians, Nigerians and Pakistanis ...' and other Indians.[9] I am not in any way 'better' than them. So why should I be able to breeze through immigration lines, while they queue and quake, always on the edge of being hauled off to airport interrogation rooms?

While musing about his decision not to apply for the Danish passport that he is eligible for, Khair says that to do so would imply that he somehow thinks of Denmark as superior to India, whereas he knows that 'the heart of whiteness is lit with lamps of blood ...' The idea of 'upgrading' one's passport to that of a rich, invariably white, country, has undertones of native informant, collaborator, Judas. Those of us born only a few decades after the end of the colonial period, are vulnerable to that effect. Or at least, I am.

Yet, there is also a part of me that is annoyed by what can feel like false dichotomies. Why can't I love India and Spain? Why can't I have two passports? The latter is more of a rhetorical question, the literal answer being that the Indian Constitution does not allow dual citizenship. India requires strict monogamy. The constitutional framers believed that multiple passports would lead to divided loyalties that would ultimately threaten the integrity of the Indian Union.

And yet, cosmopolitanism has roots in India too. It is not merely a Western conceit. India's first Nobel laureate, the poet-philosopher Rabindranath Tagore, wrote: 'I, who have the amphibious duality of nature in me, whose food is in the West and breathe air in the East, do not find a place where I can build my nest. I suppose I shall have to be a migratory bird and cross and recross the sea, owning two nests, one on each shore.'

It's as if he were writing of me, to me. I was born a mongrel: a north Indian and a south Indian, a Hindu and an atheist, an English-speaker with un-English skin, a half-caste with cultural capital. My mother's family was from the Lucknow-Allahabad area in Uttar Pradesh, but she had grown up in Bombay and Calcutta where she had been educated by nuns in missionary-run convents. Her father used to eat his rotis with a fork and knife. She read English literature at university and wore sarees with great elegance.

There was hardly a superstition that she didn't believe in: numerology, vastu (a belief in architectural principles being capable of creating positive force fields), no cutting of nails at night. She liked Krishna and Ganesha, and also used to take me to visit a small church behind Khan Market, a shopping complex in New Delhi.

My father is a Tamilian, who had been born in Gujarat. He went to school in Dehra Dun. At university in England, he spent most of his time betting on horse races and card games. That perhaps foreshadowed his becoming an economist by training. He is an atheist, a writer, a reader. He likes a good beef burger whenever he can get hold of one.

Before I began primary school, I had two 'best' friends from my neighbourhood in Delhi. One was Sadia, a Muslim who lived a few houses down from us. I remember visiting her extended family in Old Delhi on occasion. Her dad would load up her, her brother, her mother (shrouded in a burkha for the outing) and me on to his two-wheel scooter to take us there. We ate the best food at Sadia's home.

Then there was Simrin, a half-Sikh, half-American girl, with light brown hair and almost-green eyes, in whose home I saw bottled water for the first time. It was an amazing thing to me that there were people who paid for water in plastic bottles as if it were Campa Cola.

Once I began school, many of my new friends were Punjabi Hindus with immigrant backgrounds—families who had left Pakistan immediately before Partition. I learned to love the open-heartedness of their homes, the kineticism of the dancing at their celebrations and their easy generosity.

In short, I grew up in love with India, its multiplicities, and ease with contradiction. Being Indian at that time allowed me to be this complicated messy thing. It allowed me to be more and greater—instead of being reined in and tightly delineated.

I grew even more complicated as I travelled. Over the last quarter of a century, the love I had grown up with for India has expanded until I have fallen in love with the world. Beijing's hutongs, Indonesia's sambals, Brussels' antique markets, Oxford's libraries, Spain's flower-filled balconies and Tokyo's dentists—these are all joy-giving affirmations that I feel pride in. 'Look!' I want to tell people, 'Come and see these things. Aren't they glorious?'

In effect, I have collected so many identities that I feel like I am building a luminescent shell within which I shelter, snail-like. I have become a little Chinese and a little Spanish, with a splash of Japanese. I prefer using chopsticks to forks. I have embraced Spanish nationalism when it comes to wine. I have learned to eat dinner at 6 p.m., thanks to living in Tokyo and to drink hot water because of my years in China. I call French fries 'frites.' And the sentences I exchange with my husband, are in our own special patois:

> '*Chalo chalo*, aren't you ready yet?'
> '*Belum*. I can't find my *chanclas*.'

Birth is a lottery, and not everyone can fly. Political realities are grimmer than ever: asylum seekers being pushed back at sea, students denied visas over social media posts, entire nationalities deprived of the right to mobility. But sometimes, we are fettered by the mind rather than circumstances. And in that case, it's a tragedy not to soar. We all have it within us to be boundary-crossing cranes, even though it can seem as if we must fly ever higher to reach the other side.

6

REPORTING

Show a people as one thing, as only one thing, over and over again, and that is what they become.

Chimamanda Ngozi Adichie

It is 2004. I am twenty-nine years old, and staring at an avuncular Indian gentleman who is expecting an answer from me, that I don't understand how to provide. He is in Beijing to expand his business, and I am a foreign correspondent based in China. I'm working on a story on an uptick on bilateral investment and had written to him a week ago to set up this interview. I'd introduced myself as a reporter for one of India's leading English-language newspapers. And now here we are, at a cafī in central Beijing.

My interviewee repeats his question for the second time, 'What are you doing here, *beta*?' I am confused by the query in general, but I bristle, at the 'beta,' in particular. It's a common enough way in India for someone to address a younger person as 'child,' but this is a professional situation. And I am still at the age where assumptions about my youth feel disparaging.

I bite back the smorgasbord of caustic replies that play on my tongue. 'I am *not* your child.' 'What are *you* doing here?' 'Fuck off!'

Instead, I patiently explain yet again, with exaggerated slowness that I am a journalist. And that as I had said in my email to him, I am interested in learning about his investment plans for the Chinese market. But he continues to look as nonplussed as I feel. We are speaking to each other in English, but the meaning beneath the words is clearly divergent.

'You are here with your parents?' he changes tack. And only then does the penny drop.

The businessman isn't asking me about my job, his is an existential question. What am I, a young Indian woman, *doing* here in a foreign country, China. Who is securing me? He wants to know the person responsible for my presence in a place I do not belong to. In his episteme, a woman's job is her hobby. It does not suffice to explain her being out of her proper place.

For a moment I resist giving in and telling him what he is really after. But in the end, I decide I just want to get the interview started and done with. 'I live here with my husband,' I say, and immediately the man relaxes. All is well with the world after all. '*Arre, beta—to ye batana tha na?*' (Well, child, you should have said so!) He chuckles for a second and finally begins to address my queries about his plans for investment.

At the age when I was encouraged to think about what I might do when I grew up, 'foreign correspondent' didn't exist in my ontological imaginings. My father was a journalist and my mum a TV presenter, so that 'correspondent' was the wallpaper of my early years. It was the foreign part that was, well, foreign.

As a job description, the foreign correspondent is better named the 'western foreign correspondent'. For it is the rich West's reporters who have long accrued to themselves the function of being explainers of the world. The white male reporter helicoptering into war-torn parts of the globe is a sight that the international TV audience is habituated to. By the time an Indian passport holder's visa for the concerned afflicted country comes through, the war could very well be over.

From childhood, I had imbibed the sense that the proper subject for an Indian, was India. When studying for a history degree at university in the UK, for example, it was considered natural that I would take a majority of my courses in Indian history; an assumption that I complied with. Just as I had never imagined being a foreign correspondent, I had never imagined becoming an authority on British history, even though those who taught me Indian history were themselves British.

It took me dating a Spaniard at university in London to begin thinking more expansively. Julio, my future husband, believed that for an Indian to focus their learning on India was somewhat of a cheat, too easy. He had spent his undergraduate years learning Japanese and Chinese. 'Come to China with me', he'd said in that innocent, irresistible way of the passport brahmin, casually conjuring a way of inhabiting the world that I'd never considered to be mine.

I took the bait and, one serendipitous step at a time, started down the road of my lonely travels as an Indian foreign correspondent. To be this person was to be resigned to a lack of collegial compatriots. In Beijing, where I worked for most of the early 2000s, I was one of only two Indian correspondents covering China. My lone colleague was a gentleman in the employ of India's state-owned newswire, the Press Trust of India, who had spent a decade living in the city without managing to learn any Chinese.

This was a time when politicians on both sides of the Himalayas were prone to gabbling about a putative new world order that would see the 2.4 billion people of China and India joining hands in a formidable hardware–software partnership. The fact that there were only two Indian journalists in China reporting the emergence of this 'Chindian' behemoth requires explanation, as do the consequences of this paucity.

By 2008, the year Beijing hosted the Olympic Games, my PTI colleague and I were joined in China by two more Indian reporters. But to put this in context, that year there were some 700 foreign reporters resident in the Chinese capital alone, plus dozens more in Shanghai and other cities.[1]

In 2009, I moved to Brussels, home to the headquarters of the European Union, to become the only Indian journalist covering the EU in what was, according to the city authorities, the world's second-largest assembly of the foreign press after Washington DC. Next, we moved to Indonesia, where I spent four years from 2012. In the country that boasted South-East Asia's largest economy, I was once again the sole journalist writing for an Indian publication. And my lonely sojourn as Indian correspondent abroad continued in Japan.

What explains this meagreness of Indian reporters in the wider world? There are economic and logistical reasons for it, certainly. The money and visas needed for travel, research and dissemination mean that citizens of rich Western countries have long dominated the production of global knowledge.

But this isn't the whole picture. There is also the competition that foreign news in India faces from domestic stories, coupled with India's generally modest perception of its role in the world. Given its subcontinental size, the national media are deluged by huge daily stories, from billion-dollar corruption scandals and gang rapes, to the shenanigans of Bollywood stars and the fortunes of its cricket team. News about a bribery scandal in Indonesia, or a new European Union decree on customs, does not register in Delhi newsrooms. On occasions when a foreign news story is of interest, usually because it connects back to India in some way, the media runs pieces from the established (Western) news agencies like Reuters and AFP that they pay subscriptions to.

Most Indians remain focused on their internal politics and challenges, and only rarely see themselves as citizens of the world. Cognisant of global geo-strategic power dynamics, we have grown up with the idea that the proper concern of Indians is India—not the world—as common sense. The media simply reflects this general orientation. We don't need to pay attention to most of the outside world because we are not in the business of policing far-flung places, engineering coups, passing judgment on other systems of government or being horrified by their lack of human rights. We have enough to be horrified by at home and are doing a spectacularly bad job at policing ourselves.

That said, the more years I spent travelling in the role of lone Indian foreign correspondent, the more I realised that the absence of an Indian gaze on the world mattered for how this world is broken down, digested, understood and acted upon.

The traffic below moves in orderly constellations, headlights sparkling against the crepuscular sky. I am sitting on a high floor of one of the recently opened skyscrapers that have begun to line the Chinese capital's third ring road. Beijing's infrastructure never fails to shock my Indian sensibilities with its girth and confidence. How has this city of bell-tinkling cyclists in Mao suits morphed into rivers of motorists flowing down six-lane highways? There is little evidence of honking even when traffic is gridlocked. No stray cows amble across the autosphere. The discipline of Chinese drivers is something visiting friends from India never fail to remark on.

Just then a German reporter that I am sharing a sundowner with, shakes his head. 'It's just crazy, isn't it?' he asks. I am about to agree that the discipline of Chinese drivers is indeed remarkable, when he continues, 'What chaos! I doubt half those drivers even have valid licences.'

We are both seeing the same thing: Beijing traffic on a weekday evening, but we are *seeing* it in totally different ways. I am looking at something well-regulated, if slow moving. My friend is beholding bedlam. We cannot help but filter our observations through our implicit lenses, our barely conscious ideas about what is 'normal,' the benchmark against which we observe deviance.

But because there are only two of us with Indian norms reporting on China, and hundreds of others with Western ones, the world, most Indians included, learn about a China of anarchic traffic, not one of orderly driving.

It is early 2006 and I am in China's peripheral Ningxia province. Bounded on the north by Inner Mongolia, this loess-covered region is amongst the nation's poorest. I'm visiting the area with a small group of foreign correspondents, ostensibly to write about desertification. The real, if not openly articulated, reason is 'poverty reporting'. With only a couple of years to go before Beijing hosts the Olympic Games, an opportunity to show off its red-capitalist glitter, there is increasing scepticism about the face that China shows the world.

We are here to discover the 'real' hardscrabble China of deprivation and scarcity that is hidden by the smokescreen of Beijing and Shanghai's infrastructural razzmatazz. I'm often lectured by Indians—fed on a diet of western media-reported stories—that the only real difference between India and China is how the latter keeps its poverty under wraps, while we display ours on the footpaths. China, they tell me with New York Times-confidence, is equally poor, but unlike democratic India, it is not politically compelled to acknowledge this poverty.

I am therefore champing at the bit as much as any of the other foreign correspondents to finally discover this fabled destitution. As a proud Indian, I have always valued our democracy and been somewhat bewildered that an authoritarian country has, prima facie, achieved so much more than its democratic neighbour in advancing the material lives of its citizens, with all the attendant benefits for health and civic life.

So how real is China's success in poverty alleviation? A small (nationalistic) part of me wants to be able to call it a show of smoke and mirrors. In Ningxia, a French reporter assures me, I will finally find all the poverty I need to prove that China is not so different from India after all. The place where this discovery ostensibly awaits is Shuang Jing Zi, a hamlet so encroached upon by the surrounding desert that two-thirds of the village's population has moved away. Only the old and infirm are left behind. Shuang Jing Zi is part of the Ozymandian Su Bu Jing township in the province's north-west. But Su Bu Jing is no longer even classified as a township. Following two decades of depopulation, its name quietly stopped appearing on maps three years ago.

In the village, we meet with sixty-year-old Qiao Gui Yin, one of the hundred or so people who still lives there. Qiao's voice is papery-old as he talks at length about the deprivations the villagers endure. All the youngsters have left for better lives, he says. No women want to marry into this village. My colleagues busily write down every word, pained expressions of sympathy wrinkling their brows.

His son is amongst those who has gone to work in Yinchuan, the provincial capital, Qiao says. I ask him if he has been to Yinchuan himself. 'Oh yes!' he replies, face suddenly alight. 'It's a wonderful, modern city. Much better than Beijing.' 'Have you been to Beijing?' I ask. 'No, no!' he responds. 'Just seen it on TV.'

'You have a TV?' I am gobsmacked.

'Of course,' he says dismissively, swatting my question away.

Inside Qiao's dwelling I find not only a TV, but a DVD player, and standing next to his bed, an electric fan. All indications point to the fact that I later confirm: the village has an electricity connection. Outside, a newish-looking motorcycle is parked against a wall.

In India, because the definition of a 'middle class' based purely on income is notoriously complicated, many studies have instead adopted a consumption-based classification.[2] According to this, households with income that is spent not just on food and clothing, but consumer durables like refrigerators, or personal vehicles like motorcycles, are squarely placed in the middle class.

I feel slightly wretched taking in Qiao's collection of white goods, any inkling of schadenfreude snuffed out. My western colleagues are animated at his story of poverty, but all I can see is upward mobility.[3] Once again we are looking at the same thing but *seeing* different things. To me, Qiao is in no way describable as poverty-stricken. At worst, he is on the lower end of the middle-class spectrum.

There is one incident in which I find myself in agreement with other Beijing-based foreign correspondents. Towards the end of 2006, we are all equally shocked to discover that the vice mayor of Beijing, Liu Zhihua, has been sacked over bribe-taking allegations. Liu had been in charge of overseeing the USD 40 billion budget for Olympic Games-related projects. But he is now charged with bribe-taking to the tune of 10 million yuan or USD 1 million.

The difference between my colleagues and me is not in our reaction, but in what caused it. The Western journalists are shocked because of the corruption, while I am shocked that Liu has in fact been fired. Given my India-shaped implicit norms, when it comes to the politically powerful, corruption charges are as ubiquitous and about as insignificant as a buzzing fly on a monsoon day.

(In 2023, 306 or 40 per cent of India's 763 members of parliament had declared criminal cases against them, including charges of murder and crimes against women. Liu Zhihua was eventually arrested, tried and given a suspended death sentence in 2008.)[4,5]

The primary divergence in my views and that of many Western reporters is their automatic ascription of all China's ills to the authoritarian nature of its political system. But I am from a democracy and uncomfortably aware of how little this achievement has translated into better governance or less corruption. From the impunity of the powerful and the patchy application of the rule of law, to environmental destruction and yawning income inequalities, India's challenges either match, or are worse, than China's.

I feel alone in my sight, like I am the only one of China's foreign correspondents with astigmatism.

My wonky eyesight worsens in Brussels, the city that serves as the headquarters of the European Union. It's 2010 and I am seeing completely different things to what other foreign reporters observe. We are in the midst of the euro crisis, and much global newsprint is devoted to describing the fallout of years of dodgy bookkeeping in Greece. Economic austerity is being imposed across the region. Belts are being tightened. Unemployment is spiking and the headlines are filled with the word 'crisis'. But when I look around, I see coffee-scented privilege.

It is difficult to walk near one of the European Union's office buildings without encountering all manner of protest pageantry. There is drumming and even some dancing. People hold up placards that read, 'Say no to the crisis!' Despite the facile slogans, at first I find it exhilarating. China's authoritarian leaders rarely permitted public demonstrations, and the lack of audible dissent on Beijing's streets had been a deafening silence.

In Brussels, there are cows mooing at cops. Irate fishermen throw their daily catch at Eurocrats. People chant and clap. The freedom of this theatre is alluring to my China-habituated eyes. But then the astigmatism kicks in and I begin to find it harder to sympathise with the protestors.

They are not malnourished coal miners from northeast China whose families are dying from lung cancer. They are not subsistence peasants from Sichuan whose land has been arbitrarily appropriated by corrupt local government officials.

They are not tribals from India's forests whose women have been raped and leaders murdered by mining company bosses.

The bulk of these protestors are trade union–protected workers fighting against any loss of their substantial entitlements. Striking dock workers, refuse collectors, pharmacists, newspaper vendors, taxi drivers: everyone is incensed over their dire circumstances. But I wonder if they realise just how lucky they are.

In response to EU plans to gradually abolish subsidies for dairy farming, Belgian farmers dump three million litres of milk on fields around the country. India is home to more than a third of the world's 150 million malnourished children under the age of five. These wasted rivers of milk make me angry. Where others see suffering farmers, I see immorality. My lenses are wider.

In Belgium, French-speaking Walloons from the economically depressed south of the country refuse to learn Dutch, despite the availability of jobs in Flanders, the northern Dutch-speaking region of the country. And this isn't just a Belgian idiosyncrasy. I read about the town of Sélestat, on France's border with Germany. There are few jobs in this town, but plenty of work in neighbouring Emmendingen, across the border. The mayor of Emmendingen gives an interview stating that a job is available for anyone who can count to ten, with the caveat that they speak German. But his offer has few takers in Sīlestat.[6] Surely, I think, it isn't that hard to learn a language if it's a matter of livelihood.

In the spring of 2012, I visit Italy to profile Punjabi agricultural labourers—the second largest Indian diaspora in Europe. The farmhands I talk to in Latina province stress their willingness to work hard. 'Italians don't like to work too much,' Sartaj Singh, a clean-shaven Sikh lumberjack, tells me, on a late morning break from felling trees. 'They keep on going on holiday and make life difficult for the bosses.' His friend, Harbhajan Singh, pipes up: 'Before we [Punjabis] got here, the fields were barren. There was no one to work in the fields. Today if there is agriculture in Latina, it's only because of us.'

The Sikhs speak Punjabi-accented Italian with practiced ease, and when I ask them if they take classes, they burst out laughing. They have learned on the job. 'If we didn't know the language, who would hire us?' one of them says. 'We've been here ten years, madam,' another adds, 'Even an animal would have learnt Italian in ten years.'

I begin thinking the thoughts of Europeans on the right, although I identify as left-wing. People need to work harder. Privileges are not rights. You call this a crisis? It's the best-dressed, most bucolic crisis I've ever seen.

Before we depart Belgium for Indonesia, I get LASIK treatment done at a well-known eye clinic to fix my short-sightedness. The ophthalmologist warns me to have modest hopes for the outcome. The surgery will not cure astigmatism, he says.

The mosque's silhouette is blurry in the downpour. The rain in East Java tends to heavy, giving the land its paddy-green hue. It's the hour of the maghrib prayer and all 4,000 students at Pondok Modern Darussalam Gontor, one of Indonesia's largest *pesantren* (Islamic boarding schools), are gathered inside the building.

It's November 2015, over three years since I began reporting from Indonesia as the country's only Indian foreign correspondent. This visit has taken several months to arrange. Women rarely knock on these doors, foreign ones even less.

My motivation is journalistic, but my inspiration literary. I first read about pesantren in V.S. Naipaul's 1981 travelogue, *Amongst the Believers*, an account of his journeys to four Muslim countries, including Indonesia. Naipaul was cynical about the value of these schools. He remained unconvinced that their students learned anything useful and was darkly suspicious of the Islam emptied of 'local particularity' that some emphasised.

His conclusion at the end of his first visit to a pesantren, '..it wasn't tradition, and it wasn't education. It was a breaking away from the Indonesian past; it was Islamisation; it was stupefaction ...'

But I'd also read Indonesian writer, Ahmad Fuadi's, fictionalised memoir, *The Land of Five Towers*, which painted a different picture. Fuadi was a Gontor graduate. And his book centred on the four years he spent at the school in the late 1980s. It read like an Indonesian version of one of Enid Blyton's boarding school adventures, detailing the close friendships forged by pupils as they dealt with the emotional turbulence of adolescence. The author repeatedly emphasised the inspirational role the pesantren played in instilling discipline, compassion and resilience in its wards.

I'd met Fuadi at a literary festival in Bali. He was pleased that his book had piqued my curiosity. And when I asked for his help in petitioning his alma mater for permission to visit the campus, he readily agreed.

And so here I am at the crack of dawn, swatting away giant flying ants in the tubelight-lit veranda of the school's main assembly hall, waiting for the morning prayers to give out. Abruptly, a lava-flow of boys gushes down the long staircase from the mosque's upper-floor prayer room. Their slippers squelch in the wet. Prayer mats hang from their narrow shoulders.

The boys gawk at me, a bedraggled salwar kameez-clad apparition, standing in the rain taking notes. Their dark eyes are curious, but they avert their faces if I look at them directly. My chaperone at the school, a twenty-three-year-old teacher, Ustad Aliy, offers to hold my handbag as I furiously scribble notes. '*Terimah Kasih*,' I nod, using the Bahasa Indonesia phrase for 'thank you'. Aliy looks startled. I correct myself and say, '*shukran*'. I'd been pre-warned by Fuadi that in Gontor, speaking Indonesian is against school rules. The only languages permitted on campus are Arabic and English

Gontor is one amongst thousands of pesantren in the Indonesian archipelago. These Islamic schools are usually located in the countryside, and many combine scriptural learning with secular elements taken from the national curriculum. They have existed in Indonesia for centuries, but their contemporary reputation is dubious, with Islamic radicalisation having emerged as a concern world over. The question I am trying to investigate is whether they are in fact breeding grounds for Islamic extremists, as is often assumed.

Indonesia has suffered from Islamist terrorism since the start of the new millennium. The most notorious attack was the 2002 bombings in Bali, which killed over 200 people. More recently, militias in Syria and Iraq, including the Islamic State, have attracted hundreds of recruits from the archipelago. About forty pesantren are known to be associated with terrorist outfits like the Jemaah Islamiyah (JI)—the group responsible for the Bali bombings. But there are a large number that do not preach violence. All, however, emphasise a strictly orthodox, 'Wahabi,' understanding of Islam inspired by the ideas of Muhammad ibn Abd al-Wahab.

Some analysts argue, counterintuitively perhaps, that pesantren serve as a bulwark against extremism, by giving students pride in their own culture. There is research I've read that suggests it is Indonesia's secular universities that are more fertile grounds for Islamism than pesantren. Students who are unfamiliar with the intricacies of their own religion are more vulnerable to being swayed by religious 'proofs' quoted out of context regarding violent jihad. But pesantren graduates who are schooled in hadith scholarship can spot scriptural distortions. They also tend to be more connected to their communities, which gives them a stable sense of identity and consequently makes them less prone to radicalisation.

I have some sympathy for this line of argument because I am from a country, India, where secularism has not meant suspicion of religion as much as an equal embrace of all religions. The daughter of an atheist father and pan-believing mother, I've grown up singing Christian hymns and Hindu bhajans mixed in with the national anthem at school assemblies. My 'best' friend from the time I was sentient, pre-school, was a Muslim neighbour, Sadia. We had sleepovers at each other's homes. Twice a year, I was invited to her home for a special Eid celebration and drank roohafza from glasses with Arabic verses inscribed on them. Muslims are not formless bogeymen for me; empty receptacles in which to store generalised dread. Long beards do not set off alarm bells in my head. Covered heads signify tradition and respect and protection from the sun, depending on the context. I am simply not primed to be suspicious of Muslims in the way most western foreign correspondents are.

Gontor was established in September 1926 by three brothers collectively known at the school as the 'trimurti'. That this triumvirate of Muslim reformers are referred to by a Sanskrit term, literally the 'three forms,' that denotes the three Hindu gods of Brahma, Vishnu and Shiva, is an irony that is lost in Indonesia.

The term's Hindu connotations have become opaque with the centuries. They elicit no recognition when I raise the matter. I'm reminded of Naipaul's observation of Indonesians as a people who have simultaneously retained and lost their Hindu-Buddhist heritage, so that they 'talked as though they remained mysterious to themselves.'

Gontor was founded against a socio-political backdrop in which pesantren were struggling to come to terms with the gauntlet of 'modernity' thrown down by western colonialism. The trimurti derived their institutional inspiration from the venerable Al-Azhar University in Cairo, the relatively unknown Shinquit Islamic school in Mauritania, the reformist Aligarh Muslim University in India, and the Bengali-Hindu Nobel laureate, Rabindranath Tagore's experimental school at Shantiniketan.

The school curriculum includes non-religious subjects like science and history, but the emphasis is on 'foreign' languages, with English and Arabic as the sole media of instruction. The students' lives are spartan. They sleep thirty to a room and have scant belongings except a mattress, a few changes of clothes and their books. 'It is a simple life,' Aliy beams. 'Simple and sincere.' There is something cultlike about his relentless enthusiasm. Occasionally, he squeezes his eyes shut, and proclaims, 'I just love Gontor.'

By 8.30 in the morning, the sun is already harsh. The students are in their classrooms, where they stay put until noon. They'd been up much earlier though, in time for the 4.30 a.m. *Fajr* prayers, the conclusion of which I had witnessed. The hour between 5.30 a.m. and 6.30 a.m. was for laundry, bathing and eating breakfast. Naipaul had noted that pesantren 'still kept the hours of the monastery, still required day and night devotion of the inmates,' and this certainly seems true of Gontor.

I am scheduled to meet one of the school's three *kyai*, or religious heads, around noon. Before the meeting, Aliy fusses about me like a mother hen, directing me to adjust my headscarf this way and that, until it has achieved some ideal of hair-covering perfection.

My interview with kyai Hasan Abdullah Sahal starts off awkwardly. He refuses to look me in the eye. It is difficult to move the conversation beyond platitudes until Aliy mentions that the kyai had visited India in 2009. When I ask where, the sixty-seven-year-old becomes animated as he searches his memory for names. 'It was a university,' he says, snapping his fingers. 'The one where Shahrukh Khan went.'

'Surely, you mean Sir Syed Ahmed Khan? Was it Aligarh?' I counter. But the kyai only looks confused. 'I'm an old man,' he mutters apologetically. 'I forget names.' Later, a senior teacher who had accompanied the school principal to India tells me that the university in question was indeed the Bollywood hero, Shahrukh Khan's, alma mater: Jamia Millia Islamia.

Gontor is not typical of Indonesia's pesantren, the majority of which are smaller, and less well-funded. But it is possibly the most influential of the country's Islamic boarding schools, boasting an array of alumni luminaries, who collectively dominate the religious landscape of the country. Gontor graduates have held top positions at both of Indonesia's rival mass Islamic organisations, the 'traditionalist' Nahdlatul Ulama (NU) and the 'modernist,' Muhammadiyah. The membership of these two organisations numbers in the tens of millions. But while NU promotes a traditional Islam, rooted in the cultural particularities of the Indonesian archipelago, Muhammadiyah is oriented towards 'cleansing' Islam of some of its local flavour, by advocating greater scriptural adherence.

I meet with Dr Dihyatun Masqon Ahmad, one of the school's most senior faculty. He'd studied in India, at Jamia Millia Islamia (of Shahrukh Khan fame) in the early 2000s, and speaks passable Hindi. He tells me that Gontor is a paragon of belief in diversity. 'Only belief in Allah is required here,' he says, pointing out that all four schools of *fiqh*, or Islamic jurisprudence—*Shafi'i, Hanafi, Hanbali, Maliki*—are taught at the school. 'We are a meeting point for all.'

A reason why some analysts posit that pesantren serve to inoculate students against radicalisation is the concept of the contestation of ideas that emerges naturally in these schools because of this teaching of the fiqh. But there are clear limits to how much diversity is accepted at Gontor. Muslims identifying as Shi'a or Ahmadiyya, groups regarded as apostates, are not discussed. Ninety-nine per cent of Indonesia's Muslims are Sunni.

The very first story I had reported on after moving to Indonesia was about a group of eighteen Ahmadiyyas who had been holed up inside a fenced-off mosque for over two months in Bekasi, a Jakarta suburb. They had barricaded themselves inside after local police sealed the structure, placing locks on the entrances and erecting a fence around it of corrugated metal sheets.

They were refusing to come out until the mosque was allowed to reopen and serve as a place of prayer for the area's 400-odd Ahmadis. A local government hoarding referring to a number of anti-Ahmadiyya decrees and resolutions passed by religious and central governmental authorities was planted outside the mosque.

In Indonesia, the Ahmadiyya community had been declared to be religiously 'deviant' by the Majelis Ulema Indonesia (MUI), a coalition of Muslim organisations, since 2005. In 2008, President Yudhoyono signed off on a decree which ordered the community to stop all activities that 'propagated' their beliefs. The vagueness of the decree's wording emboldened some regional governments to interpret the law as an outright ban on the practice of the Ahmadiyya faith.[7]

Negotiating the considerable diversity within the Islamic fold is not the only tricky bit of ideological navigation that pesantren undertake. There is also the question of the archipelago's relationship to 'nationalism' and the nation state. Can loyalty to the nation be above that of loyalty to God? Pesantren are independent of the state and often fiercely committed to this independence. At the same time, they accept varying degrees of financial assistance from local and central authorities.

Dr Dihyatun says Gontor is proudly nationalist. 'We sing the national anthem at our school assemblies, and we believe the constitution to be the greatest gift for Indonesia.' He pauses dramatically. 'And yet, they dare come here and accuse us! They ask all these questions, as if we are terrorists.' His voice rises an octave.

In the wake of terrorist attacks in Bali and Jakarta, Indonesia's tough counter-terrorist unit had paid interrogatory visits to pesantren across the country, including Gontor. This is scarcely surprising given that the spiritual head of the country's most notorious terrorist outfit Jemaah Islamiyah, Abubakar Ba'asyir, is a Gontor alumnus from the 1950s. Baa'syir who served a fifteen-year prison term for his involvement in running terrorist-training camps in Aceh (he was released from prison on 8 January 2021), is the founder of Indonesia's most infamous radical pesantren, Al-Mukmin in Ngruki. Dr Dihyatun complains about how some journalists confuse the Gontor school with the one at Ngruki. But he also refuses to condemn Ba'asyir himself, describing the convicted terrorist as 'an old guy with his own ideas.'

It is not religion that is behind radicalisation, Dihyatun claims, but 'poverty, western imperialism, and inequality.'

I'm inclined to think that there is some truth to this explanation, overly simple though it is. I am struck by the point about inequality, which has strong resonance in a country like Indonesia, where socio-economic differences are stark. Given this context, pesantren have an important levelling effect. Regardless of background, Gontor students pay only $40 a month all-inclusive as fees. Many of them are poor boys from the sticks, but others come from privileged families. Close relatives of former Vice-President Jusuf Kalla, who is one of Indonesia's wealthiest men, have studied at Gontor.

It is quite remarkable for adolescents to have exposure to the kind of diversity of student population that the school enables, a fact that came through clearly in Fuadi's memoir, in which he describes his friendships with boys from far-flung parts of the archipelago. His closest confidants included Dulmajid, the son of a poor salt farmer from the island of Madura, and Atang, a middle-class boy from Bandung city whose parents are art-loving, government employees.

I try to think of equivalent spaces in India where the rich and poor sleep, eat and study on an equal footing. Nothing comes to mind. India and Indonesia are both riven by disparities. I have been writing a series of pieces on why popular India-China comparisons bark up the wrong tree. It is India and Indonesia that make for more relevant juxtaposition.

The fundamental challenges confronting them are similar. On the economic front, both need to boost manufacturing competitiveness to create the millions of jobs required to ensure their young and growing populations become a demographic dividend, rather than a Malthusian disaster. Both have governments that must attract foreign investment and fix creaky infrastructure, even as they assuage protectionist lobbies and battle entrenched corruption.

'*Bhinekka Tinggal Ika*' (multiple but one), the Indonesian national motto, is in essence identical to the Indian catchphrase of 'unity in diversity'. These underscore the accomplishment of having sustained national identities in societies that are fractured along ethnic and religious lines. Nonetheless, ensuring the rights of minorities remains a fraught undertaking for both.[8]

But in India, class usually trumps belief. Hierarchy remains a formidable barrier to egalitarianism. Like Indonesia, India also has tens of thousands of madrasas, or Islamic boarding schools. But the upper echelons of its Muslim demographic are unlikely to send their progeny to study there. Madrasas are synonymous with backwardness, both economic and educational. In India, they are assumed to be for children whose parents depend on the school for free meals and clothing. For children whose futures preclude medical or engineering degrees.

The fact that pesantren are classless spaces in a deeply unequal society is an angle only my Indian gaze focuses on. As I take an overnight train back to Jakarta, I am unable to rest, thoughts crowding my brain into wakefulness. In the ideological incoherence of these religious schools, the push and pull of all the competing visions of the Indonesian archipelago—nationalist, Islamist, syncretic, and radical—are present.

What I do know for certain is that astigmatism continues to be my ocular companion.

It is May 2023. I am forty-seven years old and live in Spain. I read in the news of the denial of Chinese visas to two Indian journalists who have been reporting from Beijing for the last several years.

It has been twenty-one years since I first moved to China. At the time, Sino-Indian trade stood at USD 5 billion, and there were no direct flights between the two countries. I had to take Ethiopian Airlines which flew from Beijing to Addis Ababa with a stopover in Delhi, to visit home. Since then, a lot has changed. Bilateral trade is worth about USD 136 billion, and connectivity is greatly improved. In 2019, the two countries were linked by 539 direct passenger flights. COVID led to a suspension of these, a pause that is now matched by a suspension of journalists.

It feels shocking that in 2023, the number of Indian journalists on the ground in China is back to one gentleman who works for PTI, as was the case in 2001. And even this last man standing is in imminent danger of the non-renewal of his permit.

It's all a culmination of a series of tit-for-tat measures that have been ping-ponging back and forth across the Himalayas since 2016. That year, India had four journalists based in Beijing, and Delhi was home to over a dozen resident Chinese reporters. But a deteriorating geo-political backdrop saw the unresolved India-China border becoming a flashpoint anew. Journalists are easy scapegoats, expendable. Press freedom is rhetorical flourish. It sounds good, but no one in power really wants it.

Now there is one Xinhua man left in India, for the one PTI man in China. And it is likely that neither will get visa extensions. Soon, two countries with a 4,000 km-long shared boundary, that are among the fastest-growing in the world, and that together account for a third of the world's population, will have exactly no one with any depth of understanding explaining one to the other.

Does it matter?

Some think not. Journalism is a dying profession. A majority of young people, groups of whom I teach at a university in Madrid, get their news solely from TikTok and social media influencers. Foreign correspondents are increasingly like dinosaurs, lumbering and splat in the path of an AI meteorite hurtling their way.

In the classes I teach, I continue to bang the drum of how diversity in reporting is important lest we get a one-eyed perspective on matters that deserve plural examination. But also, about how foreign correspondents don't just inform their audience back home about other parts of the world. They hold up a mirror to themselves and their home nations as well, as provocations for thought and action. Reporting on another country when done well, highlights the reporter's subjectivity to herself. The 'foreign' isn't just something to be explained, but something that helps you realise why you explain it the way you do.

Foreign correspondents are, in essence, travellers. And travelling makes it hard to 'other' the different, because suddenly it doesn't feel that different. Before I lived in China, I had believed it to be inscrutable. The scale of its architecture had felt outlandish, the language impenetrable and the art of the chopstick beyond my grasp. Once I was in Beijing, I walked the city's crisscrossing core of *hutong* alleyways. What I immediately noticed was the familiar cadence of *kabariwallahs* crying out for waste to recycle as they slowly bicycled past the faded glory of courtyard-style homes. I delighted in the spicy sizzle of street food and noted the way that strangers addressed each other as family: *ayi* (auntie), *nai nai* (grandmother), *ge ge* (older brother). Rural folk shared their boiled eggs and oranges with me on bus rides across the country, reminiscent of similar journeys in India.

Contrary to every stereotype, the Chinese people I spoke with had a ripe sense of humour and laughed often, and loudly. They also enjoyed moaning about corruption and uncaring politicians. They spat on the streets and jostled while queuing. They did not sit obediently in their seats when planes landed until the aircraft came to a halt. They often folded their hands into namastes and bowed upon learning I was Indian. 'Sakyamuni'—the Buddha—

they'd mutter. How had I ever thought this country to be alien, I'd wonder.

In 2005, I went to Turkey on my honeymoon to discover that the dessert most recommended by the locals is *halwa* (a staple in India). In Spain, I learnt that families are as boisterous, complicated and annoying as any in India. And in Belgium, I realised that the origin of French fries (Belgian apparently, not French) is as contentious an issue as the origin of a certain type of spring roll is in Indonesia and Malaysia (both lay claim to the '*Semarang lumpia*').

The world over, people complain about what foreigners have done to their food. Italians tell me there is no such thing as macaroni (the term is apparently a somewhat archaic, generic word for pasta), and Alfredo sauce is an abomination. The Spanish recoil at the idea of paella with chorizo, á la Jamie Oliver.[9] Indians are left scratching their heads at the 'Madras sauce' so beloved of British curry houses. And speaking of which, what in the name of a vindaloo is a curry house?

Travelling with an open mind, whether as a foreign correspondent or a tourist, establishes the fact that people everywhere have similar concerns. In India we wait for the rain, in Belgium people await the sun. But the celebration of "fine" weather, when it comes, is the same. In China, it is considered rude to arrive late to a party, but being early is entirely forgivable. In India, only Chinese diplomats and Huawei employees arrive before 9 p.m. for a 7 p.m. invitation. But hosts in both nations treat their guests lavishly.

Travel gives us important context. A Bruxellois inevitably groans about the terrible traffic on Chaussée de Waterloo until he encounters Beijing's third ring road. A Beijinger cannot imagine anything worse than the gridlock on Dongzhimenwai on a weekday evening until she experiences a traffic jam on Jalan Sudirman in Jakarta. And a Jakartan only need spend a weekend in Mumbai to feel a lot better about the traffic in his city.

Not everything about travel is salubrious or enriching. There are humiliating experiences at immigration checkpoints. There are moments of great frustration when you cannot be understood and cannot understand. There are limits to everyone's ability to embrace cultural diversity.

Even though there were occasions when I pretended otherwise, I never developed a taste for sea slugs in the years I lived in China. In Jakarta, I grew aggravated with my inability to find a hair salon that used warm water for shampoos. In Tibet, I ran out of inventive excuses to pass on the butter tea (not to mention yak's testicles). In Brussels, I was robbed at the airport, barely ten minutes after landing. In Spain, I was not enamoured of my dentist's insistence on kissing me goodbye on both cheeks, minutes after she had been peering into the nether regions of my oral cavity. In Berlin, I lost my luggage. In Tokyo, I lost my temper. In London, I lost my heart. But I have always gained more than I have lost.

A country should not be defined by its generals or political strategists, but by its people and their cumulative hopes and everyday preoccupations. This is what is forfeit when we lose on-the-ground foreign correspondents. In their stead, we gain Twitter trolls and professors from WhatsApp university, none of whom have actual skin in the game of hyper-nationalism and xenophobia that they engender.

Just as traveling elsewhere has the counterintuitive effect of waking the traveller up to themselves—of seeing themselves more clearly because of the comparative framework they now have—so the work of a foreign correspondent assists at a more general, nationwide level, to help a country both understand itself better, as well as its place in a wider canvas. My solitary travels as a foreign correspondent have woken me up to the astigmatism that we are all afflicted by. And to the great truth that the truth is rarely singular and always messy.

7

HAIR

Religion and commerce are equal partners in the business of hair.

Emma Tarlo

It is 31 October 1984. I am nine years old and disquieted by the congress of parents with pinched faces waiting outside the school gates. We are returning from the stadium where we've been rehearsing for the annual Sports Day spectacle. In general, I am athletically tepid. Winning a three-legged race in kindergarten has been the pinnacle of my sporting career thus far. But this day has been a treat: no classes, the weather cool after months of hot, sticky sun.

The appearance of the parents is peculiar. We still have a few hours of school to go. And their strained smiles activate an alarm, although this vague unease is mixed in with excitement as I search out my mother amidst the crowd. I run to her the moment I am off the bus, and she gathers me up in her arms so tightly that the breath leaves me. 'The prime minister has died,' she says. And then corrects herself. 'The prime minister has been killed.' I am interested. Shocked, but not unduly upset. Indira Gandhi is a lady I have watched on TV all my life, which is where she belongs as far as I am concerned—in the TV set.

We drive home through usually chaotic streets, suddenly menacing in their stillness. Even at this age, I sense a lull before the storm. For the next week, I am confined to the home. There is a curfew. At night, neighbours from our lane take turns to patrol. Sometimes, I can smell smoke in the air that wafts in through the windows. I am alternately bored and titillated by the danger that I don't quite understand.

If 'they' come, I am told we might need to make a run for it from the back window of our bedroom. Who are they? Danger has wormed its way out of my collection of adventure books and into real life. Frustratingly, it retains a chimerical quality. There are whispers of riots and I overhear someone talking of a man being set on fire. But nothing happens. I re-read an Enid Blyton series while waiting for life to start again.

When I finally return to school, after a ten-day break, my friends and I are overjoyed to see each other after the prolonged absence. We giggle and hug and jump in unison. But our chatter tapers off as one by one we notice a strange new classmate, sitting off on his own, head down. Except he isn't new, only strange, made so by the fact that the turban that had always covered his hair has gone.

We look at his uncovered head, his shorn hair. And without knowing why, my cheeks burn with humiliation. It is an awakening to hair, the tongues it speaks in, its politics. It is a chatterbox, this hair: talking of disgrace and peril as much as whispering of seduction and glory.

Sikhs made up some 2 per cent of India's population in 1984, the year of Indira Gandhi's assassination by two men who belonged to that faith. The turban is synonymous with the religion, one of whose precepts is for followers to maintain their hair uncut. This hair, according to the last of the ten of Sikhism's spiritual leaders, Guru Gobind Singh (1666–1708), must be carefully combed twice a day. Men should then tie their locks into a neat topknot covered with a turban. By maintaining their kesh (hair), Sikhs affirm that the body is divinely created, sacrosanct in its completeness.

Hair for the Sikh is vital, alive with the spirit of the divine, a soul-force. And the injunction against cutting it can perhaps be compared to the religious objection to suicide laid out by Thomas Aquinas in his *Summa Theologiae*, as an act 'impinging on the province of God.'

My classmate, a Sikh boy, had returned to school with short, exposed hair. It was as if something of his essence had been cut out of him. Haircut. The thesaurus says the closest matches to 'cut' are 'laceration' and 'wound'. There was a duality to the shame that emanated from the boy's downturned eyes. Shame at both who he was and the forced negation of that self.

The atrocities that had driven so many of India's Sikhs to obscure their identity behind haircuts, to deny themselves to save themselves, were a turning point for me. The start of a journey of learning whose main takeaway has been that to travel well is an accretive act, an embrace of more. It is the opposite of the reductive process of distilling identity until it denies all otherness—other religions, other colours, other foods, other hair.

On the morning of the last day in October 1984, while I was rehearsing for my school's Sports Day, Prime Minister Indira Gandhi had stepped out of her residence in central Delhi on the way to an interview with British actor Peter Ustinov. Within seconds she was gunned down by two of her own bodyguards, Beant Singh and Satwant Singh, both Sikh men.

Since the 1970s, the northern state of Punjab, home to most Sikhs, had been roiled by a separatist movement demanding an independent homeland, Khalistan. In response, Gandhi's administration enacted a flurry of repressive measures, which included 'Operation Blue Star'. The idea was to flush out separatists who had taken refuge inside the Golden Temple, Sikhism's holiest shrine. At least 400 people were killed in the military engagement, including civilians, and the temple complex suffered significant damage. Gandhi's assassination was revenge for this affront to the Sikh faith.

In the days that followed her death, while I read, cocooned in the safety of my house, Delhi was set ablaze. Mobs of Hindus attacked and killed every Sikh they could get their hands on, to avenge the assassination. Sikh-owned stores and homes were burnt to the ground. People were dragged into the streets and clubbed to death or lit aflame. Over 2,700 Sikhs (the actual number is contested) were murdered. Long hair made you a marked man.

In time, hair receded to the back of my political consciousness, although its aesthetic hum remained. As a fourteen-year-old, I spent hours hating my (hooked) nose, my (chicken-thin) legs, and my (boring) hair. Since only the last in this triumvirate of anatomical failings could be fixed non-surgically, I decided to focus my efforts on begging my mother for a perm. I knew that curls would make me popular, but I was also aware that parents were mysteriously obtuse when it came to knowledge of this alchemy. Surprisingly, my mother agreed, and a week after I'd asked, she took me to her hairdresser, Geraldine.

As I sat in the chair, on the cusp of beauty, my mum instructed Geraldine to give me a perm, pointing at one of the items on the style menu card. Until this day I am not sure what possessed her: whether it was lack of imagination or money, or perhaps a cruel attempt at some kind of life lesson, but my mother picked the cheapest option—a partial perm, which Geraldine obediently performed on just the front half of my head. I emerged half-poodle-half mullet-full horrendous—an hour or so later.

It was one of those moments of awfulness that creates an indelible memory, the collection of which is what we remember as our life's journey. The large part of travel is unarguably banal, but it's the occasional flashes of epiphany, wonder, horror that we retain. Post-perm, my travels in hair reverted to the mundane—shampoo, trim, rinse and repeat. It would be some three decades before I encountered truly hairy histrionics (outside of books) again.

In my teenage conviction that curls would improve my life, I'd merely absorbed widespread social ideas that have impelled women across time and space to fry, bleach, dye and wax their hair as sacrifice to a perennially unsatisfied Goddess of Beauty. What is it about hair that makes us invest so much of our selves in it? That promises to solder our cracks, heal our hurts? With the right kind of hair, we will be happier, more likable, employable, un-murderable. We know this, even as we know it is not.

Our locks are code. When shorn, they speak of grief, when long, of sexuality. When tidy, of discipline, when uncombed, of danger. These hirsute texts slot us into a sociological taxonomy: the intellectual, the snob, the wanton, the criminal.

Like many little girls, I had been entranced by the fairy tale, Rapunzel. The imagery was so bright. The quintessential blonde princess in need of rescue, had 'beautiful long hair, as fine as spun gold.' There is a corpus of academic analysis around the symbolism of hair in the story. According to one reading, Rapunzel's tresses represent an angel's halo. The length of this hair as it flows down the tall tower that she is imprisoned within, has also been described as a symbolic connection between heaven and earth. Hair is holy, virginal, precious. It works hard in the narrative.

When the evil witch responsible for imprisoning Rapunzel, learns of her hair-enabled liaisons with the forbidden prince, the punishment the witch chooses to inflict on the young lady, is to cut off her braids. With her long hair gone, Rapunzel is no longer pure; she is fallen. The damaging of women's hair as retribution for overstepping the bounds of propriety repeats itself with rhythmic regularity across the canvas of social history.

In addition to *Grimm's Fairytales*, I was also an avid consumer of *Amar Chitra Katha* comics. These garishly colored, typo-filled comic books, recounted stories from Indian mythology and folk tales. They were stuffed with boon-granting gods, curse-spewing sages, magical weapons, cunning jackals and the whole buffet of human emotions turned up to a melodramatic pitch. There was raging and thundering, lovemaking and war-mongering. I spent many white-hot, summer afternoons, travelling back into legends upon the words and images of these kathas. They were cheap. And allowed one to endure power cuts. Hair was omnipresent in them.

Sages featured top knots. Ascetics left theirs long and unkempt. Women combed their locks on riversides, attracting the fatal attention of princes unschooled in the concept of consent. In the Ramayana, an epic with profound implications for the Hindu civilisational psyche, the chatter of hair is constant. When the evil stepmother Kaikeyi wants to get rid of the righteous prince Ram, so as to make way for her own son to ascend the throne, she refuses to leave her room. She locks herself in with 'messy hair'. The idea is to guilt trip her husband, King Dasharatha, into banishing Ram to the forest. Dasharatha adores Ram and is grief stricken at being forced to send him off into the wilderness, but a wife with messy hair cannot be denied.

Later, when the monkey lord, Hanuman, goes in search of Ram's wife, Sita, who has been kidnapped by the dastardly demon king of Lanka, Ravana, the princess gives Hanuman her hairpin to pass on to her husband as token of her virtue, her peril and her love.

In the Mahabharata, the other core Hindu epic, tresses flow with as much sound and fury as in the Ramayana. When Draupadi, the wife of all five (good) Pandava brothers is assaulted by (bad) Dushyasana in front of a family gathering, her humiliation is depicted by the fact of her being dragged around by her hair. When none of her five husbands does much to stop this dishonour, Draupadi swears that she will leave her long hair uncombed and unwashed until she is revenged. Spoiler alert: it's a thirteen-year-long wait.

In the Manusmriti, an ancient legal treatise (circa 100 CE), the Hindu equivalent of Hammurabi's Code, catching hold of someone's hair is forbidden, even in a fight. (The text also states that one should not marry a woman with reddish hair, excess hair, or too little hair. But I digress). According to verse 283 of the Manusmriti, the just punishment for someone who grabs another's hair, is for their hands to be cut off.

> keśeṣu gṛhṇato hastau chedayedavicārayan |
> pādayordāḍhikāyāṃ ca grīvāyāṃ vṛṣaṇeṣu ca || 283 ||

> If he catches hold of the hair, the king shall
> unhesitatingly have his hands out off. (283)

Fast forward, and westward, to medieval Spain, and we arrive at the *fueros,* or local codes of law and custom, which mandated similar penalties for plucking someone's beard and for castrating them. Punishment for seizing a woman by the hair is also listed, although not as fearsome.

Hair was obviously not just matter. It mattered. It was seen as the seat of the soul, which explains why locks of sacred hair are believed to have healing powers in cultures around the world. Even after someone dies, their spirit lives on in their tresses. The ancient Greeks thought of women's hair as being part of their reproductive system, perhaps because of the empirical links between hair growth and puberty.[2] In this view, women without long hair could not effectively reproduce, with the consequence that hair was functionally considered to be genitalia.

It is 2024. I am forty-eight years old and watching, *The Passenger*, an opera by Polish-Soviet composer, Mieczysław Weinberg, at Madrid's Teatro Real. The story is largely told in flashback, set in a concentration camp. The staging is powerful. Much of it unfolds in a claustrophobic space, stuffed with bunks from which the limbs of female inmates emerge like so many legs of a centipede. The chorus sings of their degradation and of their desperate, irrational hope. I look at their shaved heads and although I have seen similar images many times over the years, it is different this time. I have been travelling anew in Hair, or more accurately, in hair loss, these last few months. I am attuned to follicles like never before.

It's been over a year since I was sat in my oncologist's office to discuss the post-surgical findings of my mastectomy. The doctor had been momentarily crestfallen as she'd explained that the cancer was more advanced than initial biopsies had suggested. That I would need months of chemotherapy, post-surgery, as part of the treatment plan. When I had floundered to formulate a response, she'd suddenly brightened and held up a preemptive palm, secure in her ability to allay the fear she assumed was foremost in my mind. 'Your hair,' she'd said with the triumphant showmanship of a magician pulling a rabbit out of a hat, 'will grow back.'

At this moment, in the opera house, my hair resembles those of the Jewish inmates on stage. I have recently read Primo Levi's, *If This Is a Man*, the poem with which he opens his account of living through the Holocaust. 'Consider if this is a woman,' he writes, 'without hair, without name.' The equivalence of hair and name is jarring to me, having lost my own so recently.

It takes me a minute to listen to the words without projecting my subjectivity onto them. The shaving of Jewish women was an integral part of their de-personification. Their hair, which had once sparkled with stories of love and laughter, was reduced by the Nazis to inert industrial material. Their baldness became a marker of their nothingness. When Soviet forces entered the Auschwitz-Birkenau concentration camp on 27 January 1945, they found about 7,000 kilograms of human hair packed into bales for shipment to German factories to be used in the production of felt, yarn, rope, insulators.

There are women who refuse chemotherapy even when doctors say it could save their lives. Often, they are not choosing death. They are choosing hair. To paraphrase Levi: 'Consider if I am a woman, without hair?'

On my way out of the oncologist's office on the day I was informed that I needed chemo, a nurse had handed me the phone number of someone 'very discreet'. A week later, I walked into a boxy room on the ground floor of a nondescript building in central Madrid. There was no signage outside. Inside, I detected the whiff of something antiseptic. My interlocuter was a man dressed in the white coat of a lab technician, but who spoke in the soothing tones of a practiced undertaker.

I was at a store that specialised in high-end hair systems. These are custom-made wigs, secured to the scalp with tape and glue that are worn day and night, removed only about twice a month to be washed. I was told that, if I so wished, I could return to the 'clinic' and wait in a mirrorless room while the 'prosthesis' was cleaned, so that I would never have to see myself without hair, until my own had grown back. No one, the man said sotto voce, would have to 'suspect' anything.

To have cancer could cause one to step gingerly along the streets of deception. The mother of a classmate of my younger son called me one day. She'd heard the news of my recent entry into the kingdom of the sick, a place she'd been to as well. We had coffee at my home. The mom was fuzzy on medical details like tumour histology. Having cancer was like childbirth, she said: once you were in remission, the details eluded memory.

What she did recall with enthusiasm was her hair prosthesis. 'My boys didn't suspect a thing,' she'd patted my hand comfortingly. The mom had worn the hair system round the clock while undergoing treatment. Her children were eight and twelve at the time. Keeping her illness from them had been a way for her to worry about one less thing: her kids. She asked me not to tell my son about her visit. Her own boy remained unaware that his mother was a breast cancer survivor, half a decade after the fact.

Over the next few months, my breast cancer circle expanded. The sister of a close friend was diagnosed a month after my own tumour surfaced. Next, a neighbour from my days in China reached out to introduce me to someone who had recently moved to Madrid, only to be bitten by the crab weeks later. We sent each other messages every other day, this sorority of the hair-stricken.

My friend's sister chose to try and save her locks by freezing her scalp while receiving chemo infusions. The method is called cold capping and requires the patient to wear a head covering filled with frozen gel before, during, and after the actual infusions. Cold restricts blood flow so that icing temporarily decreases the movement of blood to the scalp, reducing the quantity of toxic drugs that reach the hair follicle cells. It is torturous, but one that many women find the strength to undergo, even though there is no guarantee of its effectiveness.

'Hysterical strength,' is a term that describes the superhuman levels of physical prowess experienced by some people in extreme circumstances. Mothers have been known to fight off polar bears, fathers to lift cars, to rescue children. The explanation, although lacking scientific consensus, is that a surge of adrenalin allows a person to access physical capacities that are only unlocked under extreme duress. The fear of losing one's hair takes its place right next to the possibility of losing a child in enabling the body to endure punishment.

The other, new-in-Madrid, friend opted for a prosthesis, the semi-permanent wig. She spent some time weighing the discomfort of having an object stuck to her head for months, against having hair, even if it was someone else's. In the end, her boyfriend's opinion that she should think about how uncomfortable other people would feel were they to glimpse her bald, tipped the scale wigwards.

I chose ease. No scalp freezing, no hair system. I did buy a wig, but rarely wore it, given the heat and bother. Instead, I wrapped my bald head in colourful scarves; the debris of rarely donned birthday presents collected over the years were now upcycled into cancer headgear. My comfort level with being public about illness was high. Secrets exhausted me almost as much as the chemo.

There is no correct way to journey in illness some linger in forests of discretion. I preferred the sun-drenched plains of my blog on Substack, where I wrote myself through the process. I talked openly with my children about the diagnosis, emphasizing that little would change when it came to their routines. They could still go on play dates and attend birthday parties. Their chess and piano classes would continue. Their mother would chase them about completing their homework even from her sick bed, so no slacking off.

Sometimes, though, they witnessed me distraught, heaving with volcanic hurt. It was a process, I told them. We needed to allow ourselves to feel our sad feelings, so that they could settle into something akin to determination. I cried often, but I also laughed and sang and took pleasure in life, and books, and spring, and them.

None of which is to say that I was indifferent to beauty. In the days leading up to the start of treatment, wig shopping had provided some succour, a sense of control, a dash of silliness. The feminine pleasure of retail therapy proved cancer-resilient. Wigs, I learned, were armour to rival lipstick. They transformed and transported. Wearing one was like a short-term visa for the kingdom of the well.

The day my hair fell off, was a bad one. I had just had my second cycle of chemo, and my body felt flattened. The hair came out in tufts every time I moved my head on the pillow, even though I was too feeble to turn with any force. A day later, my husband helped me into a chair at a wig shop that specialised in cancer-related alopecia. The remaining fuzz was gently shaved off my scalp, and the sexy but affordable synthetic wig I had already picked out weeks earlier, was placed on my head. Before settling on it, I had tried, and discarded style after style. The choice was vertiginous: real hair, synthetic hair, mixed hair, long, bobbed, highlighted. As someone who likes to do their research before embarking on new travels, I began a deep dive into wigs. How had all this matter out-of-place, this hair from someone else's head, made its way into my hands?

The trade in hair is not something new. Wigs were worn in ancient Egypt. The earliest specimen, found at a burial site in Hierakonpolis dates to about 3400 BC. These hairy coverings served a dual purpose in Egyptian society, symbolic and practical, signalling high rank, while helping to protect shaven scalps (a sign of nobility) from the sun. They also aided hygiene by reducing the incidence of head lice. In more modern times, the seventeenth and eighteenth centuries were witness to an explosion of gravity-defying wiggery in the courts of Europe: think Marie Antoinette. Constructed over architectural frames and embellished with horse or goat hair, these wigs were held in place by a concoction of flour, gum, starch and a tolerance for neck pain.

But behind the finery and fashion, the dirty secret of the wig trade has always been that it relies on a gap in wealth and opportunities between those willing to sell their locks and those buying it. I read Emma Tarlow's excellent book on the subject, *Entanglement*, in which she explains why most of the hair on the global market today, is black in colour. The reason:

the main countries of origin are all Asian, notably China, India, Indonesia, Cambodia, Mongolia and Myanmar. Hair collectors in these countries are usually men on bicycles who ride around the poorer neighbourhoods, crying out their presence, although jugaadu loudspeakers are increasingly common. For women, selling their hair allows for the payment of debts, medical expenses, school fees, or just helps put some extra food on the table.

But as these nations grow richer, their citizens' need to sell hair to meet basic needs is declining. And so, it is the temples of India, especially in the south, that have emerged as the most fertile grounds to harvest locks. In Hinduism, tonsure is an important ritual of purification and renunciation. People also shave their hair to mark their mourning upon losing loved ones.

Reading the book, I was struck by just how global the trade in hair is. Tarlow visits a high-end wig shop in Chennai, where the stylist has recently returned from training in hair extensions with Balmain Hair in Paris. The shop sells products that are marketed as exotic French ones for elite Indian clients. But the hair in these has, in all probability, been sourced from India itself, been processed in China and then travelled back to its point of origin via France—a layover that bestows on it an haute couture benediction.

Over seventy per cent of the hair collected in India, from both temples and the discarded combings of ordinary folk (humans lose between fifty and a hundred strands of hair daily), ends up converted into hair products in Chinese factories. China is the biggest exporter of both human hair and synthetic hair products, with 88 per cent of the world's share in human hair goods and nearly 40 per cent in the synthetic equivalents. The United States is the largest importer of hair. China is the global mastermind of wig production. But the distribution channels of this market are more entangled. Jewish traders dominate in Europe and Israel. The billion-dollar African-American market in the US is firmly in the hands of Korean traders, while the same segment in Britain is controlled by Pakistanis.

The story of hair is rife with geopolitical rivalries. India begrudges the fact that the bulk of her comb waste hair is purchased by Chinese hair companies, who reap the value add of wig manufacture. The Chinese, in their turn, resent the Korean-American dominance of the lucrative distribution networks in the United States. And Korean-American companies see the Chinese as rivals in both the global procurement of hair and the manufacture of hair products. Adding an ingredient to this competitive congee are some African-American activists who believe it is their community that should reap the benefits of the hair extension industry in the US, that is instead feeding the coffers of Koreans, Indians and Chinese.

Tarlow also explores some of the moral panics that have historically waxed and waned around the provenance of hair. Declarations about seemingly 'innocent' hair being sourced from cadavers, lice-ridden heads, or even idol-worshipping heathens (aka Hindus), regularly erupt over the ages, upending global trade for periods of time. The authenticity of hair is a preoccupation, given the smoke and mirrors around wiggery. The hair in a wig is easily other than what it purports to be. Just because the hair you see is blonde and purchased in Russia, for example, does not mean that this is its natural colour, or that it ever grew on a Russian head. It may have started out black, been bleached somewhere in Asia, and made its way to Europe via South Africa, before entering the market as 'European hair'.

One incident of hairy hysteria that shook the world of wigs back in 2004, was dubbed 'sheitel-gate,' named after the Yiddish term sheitel, that refers to the wigs worn by married orthodox Jewish women. That year, several elderly rabbis declared the equivalent of a fatwa on the use of Indian hair in sheitels.

Religion, women and hair have a hoary relationship. It has long been the fate of women—Hindu, Muslim, Jewish, Christian—to have their tresses disciplined by patriarchs, bolstered by snippets of scripture. Men have not escaped these strictures either. As with Sikhs, Jewish and Muslim men who have divine meaning laced into their hair, both on the scalp and face. The custom of male orthodox Jews sporting beards is rooted in a biblical passage of the book of Leviticus that forbids 'destroying' beard edges and prohibits shaving with a blade. Some Jewish communities consider facial hair to be so holy that men must refrain from even combing their beards, for fear that they will inadvertently pull strands of hair out. In human society at large, hair—its length, coverings, removal—can be read as a ritualised performance of gender expectations.

The logic of the sheitel has to do with the notion that once a woman loses her virginity, her hair becomes infused with sensuality and should therefore be covered and made private, like other sexually titillating parts. The obsession with regulating hair weaves through the spectrum of human history from the Manusmriti to the ancient Greeks, on to the Prophet Muhammad, and up to the ninety-four-year-old Rabbi Yosef Shalom Elyashiv, the main driver of sheitel-gate.

The reason for the call to ban Indian hair in sheitel was ostensibly because it stemmed from idol-worshipping heathen, who were sacrificing their hair to "strange gods'.' Jewish law, *halacha*, prohibits the use of items directly involved in idolatry. The ban created havoc, leading to the creation of lists of stores selling banned wigs and the burning of wigs with Indian hair in bonfires. The economic impact ran into millions of dollars.

For many Jewish women, it was a time of moral turmoil. Although sheitel are meant to preserve female modesty, in practice, wig wearing has always been used by women to subvert through beauty. The wigs that women chose were often expensive luxury products, with styles and textures that elevated their look, allowing the wearer to be both observant and attractive. They required expensive and time-consuming maintenance to maintain their shape. In fact, sellers were often unwilling to offer guarantees on the wigs if they were not brought back to them regularly for washing and styling. As Tarlow put it, sheitel 'keeps married women's hair private but it isn't necessarily modest in style, size or effect … to wear one is a gesture of spiritual commitment but also an opportunity for aesthetic improvements.'

In the Jewish community, wigs made of natural hair were the most sought after, and those with Indian hair, the crème de la crème. According to one reading therefore, the true motivation for banning wigs with Indian hair was to make it harder for orthodox Jewish women to look beautiful, rather than the contravention of halacha.

One of the most important suppliers of hair from India for the global wig industry, was, and continues to be, the Temple of Venkatesvara, near the city of Tirupati in south India. This temple alone earns over six million dollars annually from the sale of hair that is shorn off the heads of pilgrims. Tonsure is part of a purification ritual before worshiping the image of Venkatesvara at the shrine. The hair from devotees is especially coveted by wig manufacturers around the world, for its length, lack of chemical contamination and compatibility with 'western' hair textures. Sometimes, the hair's connection to the temple allows it to be marketed as 'organic' or 'ethically sourced'.

The rabbis behind sheitel-gate however, claimed that the 'Indian' hair in wigs had been sacrificed to an idol. In fact, the hair of pilgrims at the temple is not meant as an offering to God, but is a '*mokku*,' or part of a preparatory ceremony that involves washing and other purification rites. These must be performed before a worshiper is permitted to enter the shrine. Pilgrims do not offer their hair to the deity as a gift. It is rather seen as an impurity that must be removed and discarded.

Tarlow imagines the way in which a liberal rabbi might have interpreted the hair of Hindu pilgrims ending up in the sheitels of orthodox Jewish women as divine recycling. God required some folk to take it off and others to put it on, leading to cosmic balance. 'An unspoken pact between women of different faiths and nationalities who had without knowing it, found ways of expressing their devotion and humility through sharing the same hair.'

I hadn't known about sheitel until I read *Entanglement*, but hair covering was a familiar practice to me and one I had written about in the past, especially during the years I reported from Indonesia. Although just under 90 per cent of Indonesia's 242 million citizens identified as Muslims, the popularity of the hijab, or jilbab, as it was locally called, was a relatively new phenomenon. Historically, headscarves in Indonesia were worn by older women who had completed the haj pilgrimage. These coverings tended to be loose and gauzy, unlike the opaque, ear- and neck-covering, scalp-fitting jilbab that had begun to be popular since early in the millennium.

Under the dictatorship of General Suharto (1967–1998), the Indonesian state had directed its coercive apparatus towards regulating religious symbols, including a ban on jilbabs in educational institutions. The injunction was not inspired by any feminist feelings that Suharto may have harboured, but by the fact that he saw Islamic groups as a potential challenge to his continued rule.

It was after his downfall in 1998, that jilbab-wearing began to spike. By the time I lived in Jakarta, the archipelago had been a democracy for fifteen years. And three-quarters of Muslim women and girls had begun to wear a headscarf. A Human Rights Watch report found that thirty-two local administrations across the country required a jilbab to be worn in state schools and government offices, despite shaky legal footing for any such rule. When it came to covering women's hair, the line between encouragement and enforcement was becoming so thin that it was on the verge of disappearing altogether.

As in the case of the sheitel, the significance of the kerfuffle surrounding jilbabs was not easy to unpick. On the one hand, the headscarf was associated with the end of an authoritarian regime; with the flowering of democracy and choice. A large jilbab fashion industry had also sprung up, so that for many women, headscarves and sexiness were not mutually exclusive. On the other hand, the jilbab was an import from the Middle East without indigenous cultural roots in Indonesia. And the Islamic headscarf is not just another outfit, like a skirt or a blouse. You don't decide not to wear it if it's particularly humid, or you'd simply prefer not to on a given day. Encouraging it was a conservative move that reduced the self-determination of women. Women in Indonesia were choosing to wear the jilbab, according to one line of reasoning. But could 'choices' that were the result of social and religious pressure be properly termed thus?

A few years later and the hijab reared its covered head across the Andaman Sea, in India. The different contexts in which the Indonesian and Indian hair-covering debate raged, made for a complex comparison. What transpired in India was as follows: In February 2022, several educational institutes in the southern state of Karnataka began to enforce a headscarf ban on the grounds that hijabs violated uniform dress codes. For someone unfamiliar with India's recent socio-political direction this could seem like an exemplary move—something that Indonesian schools might take note of.

But the restriction on headscarves in Karnataka's colleges was not the kind of progressive move that it might appear to be to the naïve eye. Rather, it was the product of radical Islam's equally hateful twin, Hindutva. This latter ideology's raison d'être was to cleanse India of her multicultural heritage, by either dispatching Indian Muslims (who formed 14 per cent of the population) to neighbouring Pakistan or by forcing them into cultural submission to 'Hindu' mores—mores that were defined, conveniently, by the proponents of Hindutva.

The ban on the wearing of hijabs by female students therefore, needed to be set within the wider context of Hindu nationalist antipathy towards the minority Muslim community. In the years preceding the ban, Muslims in India had been increasingly subject to moves aimed at forcibly bringing their diet, dress and other customs in line with that of the Hindu majority. These attempts enjoyed both tacit and overt political support from the national government and its regional lieutenants.

The claim that supporters of the hijab ban made regarding the need to liberate public centres of education from religious symbols rang hollow. The founding ideals of the modern Indian state included the term 'secular'. But the word had different connotations here than in a nation like France, for example, with its cherished concept of laïcité. In France, the public sphere is bleached of religion. But India is a deeply religious country where secularism equates equal respect for different beliefs rather than a wholescale restriction of belief to the private realm. In the school I attended in New Delhi, we celebrated the religious festivals of all religious communities. We dressed up as sufi quawals or angels depending on the occasion. We marked everyone's birthdays: Guru Nanak's, the Buddha's, Christ's and Krishna's. In our morning assemblies we sang Mahatma Gandhi's favored bhajan, *Raghupati Raghav Raja Ram*, mouthing 'Ishwar Allah Tero Naam,' (Ishwar and Allah are both God's name) so often, it felt like an utterly unremarkable sentiment.

In the decades since, the rising tide of Hindutva has meant that this multireligious tapestry is fast being homogenised, with Hindu cultural symbols bestriding the country like behemoths, reminding people of 'legitimate' ways to eat, dress and pray. The supporters of the hijab ban in Karnataka's schools and universities tended to be entirely comfortable with this phenomenon. It was disingenuous, therefore, cherry-pick markers of minority Muslim identity as problematic on the grounds of secularism.

In India, the irony was that those who protested the ban were more likely to be secular in their personal lives than its defenders. The hijab row was more confounding for liberals in India to negotiate than their counterparts in Indonesia. For the latter, the liberal values of feminism and equal-opportunity education meshed more easily. But in India, demanding the right of female students to wear a headscarf sat uncomfortably with the fact that the hijab was conceptually related to patriarchy. Many of the girls clamouring to be allowed to wear it were likely under pressure from their families to do so. But denying girls the chance to get an education and further their life opportunities ranked higher on the long list of regressive behaviours in India, than wearing the hijab. Liberals there argued that they were opposing the greater problem, even if it meant ignoring the smaller one. It was an uncomfortably slim tightrope that they had to walk.

Hair is complicated. Covering it has stood for choice and identity as often as it has for oppression and coercion. It has been weaponised by democracies and autocracies, conservatives and liberals. Is the hijab a choice or an imposition? Ultimately, abstracting principles—and hair—from their situated reality may help win a college debate but is empty of substance. Fighting against the imposition of the hijab in schools in one context can be as valid as standing up against its ban in another.

This is confusing to those who prefer neatness. But travels in history and culture always reveal that the truth is as unruly as a particularly bad case of bed hair.

It is September 2023. A cheer ripples around the salon, as D.R., my Argentine *peluquero* in Madrid, whips the protective cape off my shoulders. My freshly trimmed hair is the subject of this appreciation. There is so much to be said about this hair in this moment, scant in quantity but abundant in allegory: it is defiant and tenacious and most of all, it lives! It's been over nine months since my locks fell out during the second cycle of chemo; four months since the end of treatment. I haven't known

D.R. for very long, but he has followed my posts on Instagram. After I'd uploaded photos of me trying on different wigs, he sent a private message about having been on a 'similar journey' himself. 'This haircut,' he says, 'is an achievement.' There is no charge. Cancer is community.

A couple of months ago, my breast was reconstructed, but it is only with this trim that I feel as though I have returned from the other place. Over the next few weeks, I am regularly complimented on having dared to go so short. 'It's chic,' people declare. 'You can pull it off with your cheekbones.' Random women confide in me about how they've always wanted to hack it all off but lacked the courage. I smile. I nod.

I use my hair as a pedagogic tool in the classes I teach at a university. The introductory lecture is on cognitive shortcuts, or the frames through which humans organise and process information. You look at my hair through the frame of fashion, I tell my students. I know it through the frame of ill health. It's a Rorschach test.

Time ticks on and I realise that I truly enjoy my hair short. I do have the cheekbones for it. And it gives me the greatest gift—more time. A pixie is the productivity hack that always hid in plain sight. If women seemed like they juggled more balls than men, cutting off their hair eliminated more than one—washing time, drying time, styling time, trying-to decide-whether-or-not-to-exercise-because-then-your-hair-would-be-greasy-but-you-have-no-time-to-shampoo time.

I spend some of these additional moments looking at people's heads with more interest than is perhaps seemly. I feel surges of empathy for bald men in the cold. I play guessing games of 'Is it a Wig?' while riding on the metro. I am intrigued by the different ways that Muslim women shopping at the luxury stores along Calle Serrano tie their hijabs.

It's a revelatory place to travel in, hair.

8

GRIEF

No worst, there is none. Pitched past pitch of grief,
More pangs will, schooled at forepangs, wilder wring.
Comforter, where, where is your comforting?

Gerard Manely Hopkins

It is 1985. I am ten and burning up. One moment I was fooling around with my best friend at her house in Delhi. We were Madonna, lip-syncing to *Like a Virgin*. And a minute later, my head began to spin. I collapsed on the sofa in the living room, frightened, uncomprehending of the flushing and nausea. The only clear thought that pierced the fug: Mama. I want my mum.

An hour later, I am home, lying in the double bed I have shared with my mother for the last couple of years, since the divorce. She's been called at work and is on her way. I thrash about, feverish, tense. Waiting. Waiting. And then, she is there. A cool hand on my forehead. A glass of water raised to my lips. Fingers dialling the doctor. Voice concerned, but calm: 'Pali has a high fever.' And then, I stop following the conversation, because my muscles relax. They no longer need to be alert. I give myself over to sleep knowing that all will be well. My mother was home.

It is June 2023. I am forty-seven and rushing to get dressed in my bedroom in Madrid. It has only been a month since the chemotherapy finished, and I am still bald. As I try and tuck in the loose ends of the turban I have fashioned from a cotton scarf, the intercom buzzes. It's my dad and his girlfriend. They are visiting for a couple of days on their way back to the US, where they live, from India, where they have been travelling. My husband calls out to say that he will go downstairs to let them in. 'OK,' I reply, voice raised so that I can be heard across the hallway.

I am somewhere between smoothing down my shirt and giving the turban a last adjustment when the phone rings. Not now, I think. Not now, I am busy. I toy with ignoring the call. My father will be at the door any moment. But then I glance at the number, and it is my uncle, who rarely phones. I decide to answer it quickly, just to say that I can't talk.

'Hey,' I say breathlessly. 'Everything okay?'

'Pali.'

'Yes?'

'She's gone.'

Gone. She. Gone. Has.

Two syllables. And that's it.

I am on the floor, gasping. Drowning in air.

The apartment door bursts open, my father beaming, his arms outstretched. 'Pali!' he smiles, the next word frozen on his lips as he takes in my face. Wild, I imagine, when I try and recall the scene later. Bleeding animal-like. I don't remember what I say. How does one say the incomprehensible? I know that afterwards I repeat, 'I don't know what to do,' over and over again, like a mantra. Like a phrase she might utter while passing the beads of her japmala between her fingers when at her morning prayers. But she is gone.

I had spoken to her the evening before. And now she is gone. The last thing she said to me, 'Let's talk tomorrow.' I don't know what to do. What is Gone? Where is it? How can someone be alive and then be gone? One imagines that crossing heralded by some kind of cosmic cry. But it's only a distractedly answered phone call. It will never be well again, because the only person who can kiss and make it better is dead. I don't know what to do.

Whatever happens from now on, will happen in a world without her.

I was nine years old, in grade 5, when my first published work debuted in our junior school magazine, *Sandesh*. The piece in question was a poem, titled: My Mother.

Three days after she's gone, I am scratching at the insides of the stainless-steel Godrej almirah that has stood like a sentinel in the corner of her bedroom for decades. The creaking of the cupboard's door is the sound of my childhood. I was never allowed unfettered access to its treasures: layers of saris, shawls, jewellery, cash, presents meant to be recycled, vaccination records, the collected artistic output of my primary school years: drawings, including that of a peacock that won third prize in second grade, and the poem. Now finally, I have the key to this, my mother's lair. And I don't want it. But I have it. And so, I have opened the cupboard and am sifting through everything, trying manically to get at the poem. The poem not thought about for almost forty years, until it resurfaced on the flight home with an urgency that is the irrational core of grief. I could only remember the first two lines, 'I have a dear mother, who is pretty, tall and rare'. I knew there was a 'stare,' somewhere in there, for the rhyme.

I start shoving clothes off the rack, onto the floor. Convinced that if I find the poem, my mother will come back. It's not a conscious thought; more a bodily compulsion. My younger son, his eyes round as saucers, stands next to me, aware that I am somewhere very distant from him. He leans into the almirah and sticks his nose into the pile of silk and chiffon saris. 'These smell of India,' he says, and I dissolve.

Eventually, the poem is unearthed.

My Mother

I have a dear mother
Who is pretty, tall and rare
She dresses very carefully
And makes people stare
I know you won't believe it
But she has jet black hair
When she walks through the streets
The people start running
To ask her for her autograph
But my mother is very cunning
She coolly steps to the side
Says, meet you later
But only if you become a Taj Palace waiter

My mother was a celebrity. In the 1980s, she was what we would today call, 'an influencer,' ruling the screens of hundreds of millions of Indians. This was the epoch of terrestrial TV, before the advent of cable and long before streaming was anything other than a verb that applied to rivers. To tears. The entire nation tuned in to the state-owned channel, Doordarshan. And every other evening, they would encounter my mother reading the news in English at 9 p.m. She dressed in a sari and wore a bindi; spoke in a starched accent and read out government-sanitised events that were heavy on grainy footage of dignitaries—from a teleprompter, and sometimes from pages of paper, when the teleprompter failed.

In 1980s India, the news, dull as it was by today's frenetic standards, was about as exciting as watching TV could get. The alternative was Krishidarshan (literally: agricultural tour), a one-hour daily programme about the latest in seed technology. Television was only broadcast for a few hours a day, starting at about 6 p.m. The minutes leading up to it going live displayed the channel's oddly mesmerising logo—something that looked like an arthritic supernova glitchily expanding to fill the screen to the dirge-like tune.

Discussing what newsreaders wore was staple conversation between ladies getting their hair done in beauty parlours. My mother's face was up on billboards advertising everything from Marmite to TV sets. One advertisement tagline for a 'colour TV set' that featured a close-up of her visage read, 'If the eyelashes of the newsreader are clearly visible … it must be Solidaire.' We received bags of fan mail every week, many featuring marriage proposals.

Yellowing pages drop out of a folder stashed away at the bottom shelf of the almirah. They are fan letters, scores of them, creating a cacophony I can't at this moment listen to. But a few speak, before I can shut them up by shoving them back into the file.

Yesterday you looked absolutely beautiful and you read the news superbly.

Will you put on earrings? I think it will give you additional beauty.

Kumar
Calicut 1984

I used to see the news at 9.30 PM. When you are on TV screen, it is a golden chance of seeing your magic and beautiful existence. I am fall in your love. I cannot live without you. I want to marry you.

Renavikar Uday Kumar
Ahmednagar, 1988

Dear Aunty Geetanjali,
My name is Bonabelle Alice Zuzuarte. I see you very often on TV and our whole family likes to hear you read the news. I am in Std III. I like you very very much. I do not go to sleep till the news is over, specially when you read the news.

Bombay 1985

My parents divorced in 1982. I was seven at the time and divorce was very rare. I was the only child from a 'broken home,' as it was called, that I knew of. There was shame in this state, but it was a disgrace somewhat mitigated by my mum's star status. After the divorce, my mother and I moved into her father's home, where we shared a bedroom for years. The décor was dictated by me. The Godrej almirah remained a constant, but the scenes on the wall it faced changed with the passing of the years, from Snoopy posters to Duran Duran ones. It was only after my grandfather passed away, when I was in my last year of high school, that I moved into a room of my own. That she got a room of her own.

News-reading was a part-time occupation that while glamorous, did not pay enough to raise a family on. To make ends meet my mother began a full-time job as a sales executive at a chain of five-star Hotels: the Taj Group. Her office was located in the flagship property, The Taj Palace Hotel.

When she walks through the streets
The people start running
To ask her for her autograph
But my mother is very cunning
She coolly steps to the side
Says, meet you later
But only if you become a Taj Palace waiter

Fierce and feminist. My mother. Who once people would run after for an autograph. Decades before her broken foot. And the magic jar of happiness.

I love you most from amongst the news readers. I have one suggestion just out of inquisitiveness as to how you would look more cuter if you wore your bindi elongated (which would suit your face more) instead of round.

B. Narayan
Bombay, 1984

At the memorial service held in Delhi, my brother paraphrases Auden in his eulogy:

> She was my North, my South, my East and West,
> My working week and my Sunday rest

And so, it had been for me. She was my history; my memory. The reason why I liked the cushions on the sofa angled just so. Why I never pinned my sari pallus to the blouse. Why I sang *ari kukku jari kukku* to my boys at bedtime and forbade everyone from cutting their nails after sunset.

There are few dry eyes in the enormous crowd that fills the room, even though we have barely had time to cobble this gathering together. My brother flew in from the US yesterday, my family from Madrid. We cremated our mother a few hours later, at the electric crematorium, only a short distance from the neighbourhood where she had lived. HAD. I spent the short ride in the hearse next to the *body*, delirious with jet lag and heartache, thinking about verb conjugations. Why were they so complex in Spanish and so much easier in English? Había, tenía, tuve, he habido—I began reciting Spanish verb tables in my head and then—slam! She's dead. The thought was a slap across the face.

It was so very hot, the temperature in the high 40s centigrade. And yet, there were so many people who had come. Familiar faces, reaching out sympathetic arms. How had they known to be here? How were we all here, when she was gone. At some point we were at the mouth of the incinerator. A priest was incanting Sanskrit mantras that I didn't understand. As the male survivor, my brother was at the receiving end of the priestly instructions about what offerings to place and where to step. He asked the pundit, 'What about my sister?' The priest was nonplussed for barely a second before directing me to place my hand on my brother's shoulder, to connect me to the rituals that 'the boy' must perform. I should have protested. Made some kind of point about gender equality and the patriarchy. Instead,

I clasped my brother's deltoid, weakly grateful that I didn't have to pay heed. There were Spanish verbs to memorise.

At the very moment the body, *the body*, was about to enter the incinerator, the pundit asked my brother something. He didn't understand. His Hindi was rustier than mine. There was some back and forth and finally my brother leaned towards me, exhausted, 'What does this guy want? What is he *saying?*' I snapped to attention; grammatical musings paused and looked inquiringly at the priest who also looked exasperated. 'A donation, please,' he said baldly, 'dakshana'. A bribe. The priest was asking for a bribe. He wanted money before saying the final incantation that would ostensibly pack off my mother to her next life with spiritual benediction. Who could say no at this moment? My brother stuffed some cash in the man's hand. I found it all obscenely funny, so that as my mother's dead body entered the oven, I was giggling.

It was saved by the Buddhists chanting in the corner. My mother was a Hindu, and also a Buddhist. For three decades she had spent several hours a day chanting sutras. On occasion, she had wanted me to join her in her spiritual endeavours. But I always refused. When I first told her about my cancer diagnosis, she had responded by saying that she would up her chanting. I'd been infuriated. I didn't need chanting. I was going to have chemotherapy. I needed not to have chemotherapy.

Now, I want to take the irritation back into my being. I want to chant with her. I want her to chant for me.

The Buddhists had apparently not left the house since my mother was brought back, dead, from the hospital. In groups of two, people had stayed out in the living room, chanting. And at the crematorium, their voices filled the open space, lilting over the sordid demand for a bribe.

Later, I thanked people for coming. There were so many people. Someone urged me to drink a glass of water. 'It is very hot,' she said. 'You will get sunstroke.' Practicality is balm to grief. The body needs attending to, even while the mind goes journeying through the strange rabbit holes to a place of derangement. The early twentieth-century American etiquette writer Emily Post has a section on bereavement in her, *Etiquette In Society, In Business, In Politics, And At Home.* The chapter on funerals describes the bereaved as, 'not only upset mentally but all unbalanced physically.' The instructions she gives to the reader range from the moment of death to funeral arrangements. They are archaic, focused on drawn curtains and servants serving broth, removed from the now by time, class and culture. But in their matter-of-factness, they have something to offer about how to travel through the first stage of loss.

> 'At no time does solemnity so possess our souls as when we stand deserted at the brink of darkness into which our loved one has gone. And the last place in the world where we would look for comfort at such a time is in the seeming artificiality of etiquette; yet it is in the moment of deepest sorrow that etiquette performs its most vital and real service.
>
> 'All set rules for social observance have for their object the smoothing of personal contacts, and in nothing is smoothness so necessary as in observing the solemn rites accorded our dead.
>
> 'It is the time-worn servitor, Etiquette, who draws the shades, who muffles the bell, who keeps the house quiet, who hushes voices and footsteps and sudden noises; who stands between well-meaning and importunate outsiders and the retirement of the bereaved; who decrees that the last rites shall be performed smoothly and with beauty and gravity, so that the poignancy of grief may in so far as possible be assuaged.'

Post advises for carers to urge 'the ones in sorrow,' to sit in a sunny room, if possible, by a fire. 'If they feel unequal to going to the table, a very little food should be taken to them on a tray. A cup of tea or coffee or bouillon, a little thin toast, a poached egg, milk if they like it hot, or milk toast. The cook may suggest something that appeals usually to their taste—but very little should be offered at a time, for although the stomach may be empty, the palate rejects the thought of food, and digestion is never in best order.'

Across cultures, the death of someone sparks a preoccupation with food—with feeding the grieving. In Hindu tradition, there is to be no cooking for thirteen days in a home where someone has passed. The kitchen idles while extended family and friends send in food. Cooking, an act tied to life and nourishment, is paused to honour and acknowledge the gravity of what has happened—to give it a special limbic status that recognises its extraordinariness. Ordinary matters like food become part of the larger community's concern, signalling that the bereaved are not isolated in their grief. Food is physical nourishment, the provision of which balances individual sorrow with collective support, enforces ritual discipline and maintains community ties.

But my brother and I are peculiar. We are not in Delhi for thirteen days. Our lives are elsewhere. We lack faith. We are missing rites and roots. My mother had been my rites and roots. At the moment of my departure from her house, after the visits I made to see her, she'd place a vermillion dot on my head, sticky with grains of rice, and feed me a tiny bit of sugar. I humoured her with what I considered to be a bit ridiculous, knowing it was an expression of her love. I realise now that I can't explain the significance of all of it and this inability terrifies me.

While writing this, I desperately ask Grok, Twitter's AI.

1. *Vermillion Tilak*
    - *Symbolism: Vermillion is an auspicious substance in Hinduism, symbolizing blessings, protection, and divine favor. Applying it to the forehead (typically between the eyebrows, the location of the ajna chakra) invokes positive energy, wisdom, and spiritual strength for the journey ahead.*
    - *Purpose: It's a way to seek the blessings of deities—often Lord Ganesha (remover of obstacles) or Goddess Lakshmi (for prosperity)—to ensure the journey is safe, successful, and free of hurdles.*

2. *Rice*
    - *Symbolism: Rice is a symbol of abundance, purity, and sustenance. Including rice in the ritual signifies a wish for the traveller to have all their needs met—whether material, emotional, or spiritual—during their journey.*
    - *Cultural Role: Rice is often associated with prosperity and growth in Hindu rituals (e.g., it's used in weddings and housewarmings). Here, it represents the hope that the journey leads to fruitful outcomes.*

3. *Sugar*
    - *Symbolism: Sugar embodies sweetness and positivity. Adding it to the ritual reflects the family's desire for the journey to be pleasant, harmonious, and filled with good experiences.*
    - *Spiritual Undertone: It may also subtly invoke a sense of goodwill and divine grace, ensuring the traveller is surrounded by kindness and ease.*

Ritual Context

This practice is typically performed by a family member—often a mother, elder, or spouse—as the person prepares to leave. It's a small but meaningful gesture, often accompanied by prayers, mantras, or simple blessings like 'Shubh Yatra' (safe journey). The tilak is applied with the right hand, and sometimes a few grains of rice mixed with sugar are pressed onto the vermillion to stick, symbolizing the layering of these good wishes.

Broader Significance

- *Protection: The ritual acts as a spiritual shield, safeguarding the traveller from misfortune, evil influences, or unexpected challenges.*
- *Auspicious Beginnings: In Hindu belief, starting any endeavor with auspicious markings and offerings ensures it aligns with cosmic harmony (dharma) and divine will.*
- *Emotional Bond: It's also a tender expression of love and care from the family, reinforcing emotional support as the person steps into the unknown.*

No one is going to do these things for me again. Protection, Auspicious Beginnings, Emotional Bonds—all gone, like her, with her.

People say she is in heaven. Or that she is transformed into energy, a presence that I should be able to feel. In my dreams; in the prickling of my skin. A friend says her mother comes to her in the form of the colour red. Another reveals that she simply refuses to believe her mother is dead and chooses to talk to her in her head as if she were alive, in a willed act of constructive schizophrenia.

But I am terribly rational, condemned by scepticism to remain spiritually unconsoled. I try and conjure up red in my mind's eye, and all I see are Chiharu Shiota installations. Art, albeit transcendental, but no mother. My dreams are equally motherless. People with faith tell me they cannot understand how someone without it can bear to lose a beloved, can bear to be alive, to be human. But I must bear it. I must make sense of it.

I am a traveller. And will undertake this journey of grief as well as I can, knowing that reaching the destination will not soothe the hurt that sits granite-heavy in the pit of my stomach. That even at travel's end there will be no cool hand on my forehead making a reassuring call to the doctor. Yet, I know that travel edifies, although sometimes, the learnings are obscured by the force of difficult emotions so that it is only long after journey's end that its purpose becomes apparent. In Grief, we travel through the bleakest part of mid-winter. But like all seasons, winter too has its wisdoms and to winter well, means to observe its cold ways and open oneself to the potential for the transformation that comes from unravelling. From being cracked open so that the light can enter.

Was it Rumi who said this? Or Leornard Cohen?

Does it matter?

I'd first heard of kintsugi, the Japanese art of repairing ceramics, years before we moved to Tokyo and I took classes to learn the technique. A meme had been doing the rounds on Facebook with the picture of a grey bowl marked by snaking golden tributaries, and the words: 'Japanese repair broken pottery with powder gold lacquer to highlight imperfections, not hide them.'

Unlike other methods of repair like welding or gluing, kintsugi refuses to disguise the brokenness of an object. It does not aim to make what is damaged as good as new, but by making the cracks luminescent, it transforms the object into something different, arguably more valuable. Kintsugi inscribes an artifact's story in its body: the moment of the breakage, the fact that it was loved enough to be repaired; that it is likely to be handled with care in the future. All of this is written into the veins of gold and lacquer that streak across once-broken things.

In loss and illness, depression and anger, fights with spouses and unhealed hurts from childhood, all humans break, again and again. Our real stories reside along these fault-lines. Like a ceramic cup repaired using kintsugi, it is our fractures that make us incandescent. Our humanity is revealed in vulnerability, in damage.

Gratitude is a skill. Happiness is a skill. And so is grief. It has its own geography, one that the traveller must pay close attention to. To travel wisely needs time. To rush is merely to move. The good traveller must remain curious and open, present, even if the terrain is tough. Climbing to the top of a mountain or trekking through humid tropical forests is not pleasant. It needs stamina. It requires courage. But the act of making it through clarifies, prioritises, telescopes the extraneous into the essential. One step in front of the other. Breathe. Stop. Look. Feel. Breathe.

I read Katherine May's book, *Wintering*, about weathering life's difficult seasons by acknowledging feelings of pain or grief as a need, not a luxury.

> Winter requires a kind of metronome that ticks away its darkest beats, giving us a melody to follow into Spring. The year will move on either way, but by paying attention to it, feeling its beat, and noticing its moments of transition … we can get the measure of it. And if we resist the instinct to endure those darkest moments alone, we might even make the opportunity to share the burden, and let a little light in.

I share the burden with my family, even the little one, Nico, who is only just turned twelve. Six months earlier I had taken my boys along for the ride across Cancer and Chemotherapy, and now I hold tightly on to their hands as I plunge into Grief.

The cremation could not have been easy for them. They had never been to India in June's heat; never been exposed to the religious trappings of Hindu mourning, with its mix of the sublime and sordid: the bribe-seeking functionaries and hangers-on at the crematorium, the final push of the corpse into the electric oven, the overwhelming generosity of family and friends in the event of a death. Long-lost cousins holding you in an embrace that won't let you fall. The poojas. The fragrance of the flowers and agarbatti. The huge nani-shaped absence hanging over it all.

Later, I learned that some had questioned the propriety of bringing children to the crematorium. That it might have been better to leave them in air-conditioned comfort at home with Netflix to soothe their frazzled nerves, rather than exposing them to the trauma of a funeral. But then how would they learn to grieve? To be sad. To accept. The journey through Grief leaves scars. But the gifts that travelling here bestows are empathy and resilience, the qualities I would like my children to be described by above most others. If I can teach my boys to embrace difficult feelings, to stare them down, I will have been a good parent.

At the time, I don't think these things actively. My thoughts are too disorderly. The ground has flipped to the sky. But I feel them as an intuition that cuts through the morass of loss. And so, I am adamant that the children be present. That they see my tears. And watch her body. That they realise how important their grandmother had been to so many people.

I am inundated with messages from strangers. On Twitter, the trolls have fallen silent and instead there is this outpouring of nostalgia as the news of my mum's passing spreads.

'I have such fond memories of Your mom and the newsreaders who shaped the face of television and news journalism. Nation builders!'

'Your mum was a legend. Articulate, dignified. She signified a different news experience when the anchor delivered the news and wasn't the news themself, yet we knew and thought much better of them.'

'She redefined grace and elegance and professionalism. We learned our English listening to her.'

'RIP Gitanjali. You added an Indian eloquence to spoken #english that will remain etched forever.'

At the memorial service, my newly minted twelve-year-old stands up and gives a speech.

'Every year my Nani came to visit us in May, no matter where we lived in the world to celebrate my birthday together. And that was not to escape the heat in Delhi, but because she loved us. Dearly.'

We return to Madrid after a week in India during which I fail at everything: to have a death certificate issued, to find the keys to her bank locker, to figure out what to do with her car, to get on with life, which is now Grief: a gravity-free zone, a floating dead weight. Untethered, undone, unravelled. The sorrow sticks insistent to the body, like a shadow, lengthening and shortening through the day, but attached to the heels even as I try and kick it off. Metaphors are what's left to make sense of this vertiginous unreality. Were I to poke my finger into the air around me, it would stretch like latex. Grief is like Alice in

Wonderland drinking a magic potion. As Joan Didion put it, it's a world of 'magical thinking'.

I cry much of the time. No one tells me not to. My mother is dead. Why wouldn't I cry? The boys know this. Tears are nurses, tending to me, stroking my cheeks. Grief is not a pathology; it is the stuff of love.

One afternoon, perhaps four days after I am back in Spain, I recall the Magic Jar of Happiness. Every evening of November 2022, this glass jar would fill up with notes written in my mother's pearly handwriting. The love that imbued each note had been four and a half decades in the making, refusing to be dented by time or denuded by teenage rebellion or lessened by distance. It was lioness love. Broken-ankle-be-damned-love.

Six months earlier, in early November 2022, my mother had emerged from the Madrid airport in a wheelchair. I had recently been diagnosed with breast cancer and was scheduled for a mastectomy. She had insisted on coming to be with me, despite my protestations that there was no need. The day before she was scheduled to fly, she had tripped and broken her ankle, something she omitted telling me about until our meeting at the airport arrivals hall. When I first saw her hobbled and fragile, I'd felt a flash of irritation at her irrationality. Why had she come in this state? How was she going to look after me? We would now have two patients at home: my mother and I. And even at the best of times, Muma was infant-like when outside of her India comfort zone. She was baffled by microwaves and felled by Wi-Fi passwords.

The surgery took place two days after she arrived. My boys took care of their grandmother, while my husband stayed with me at the hospital. They operated the microwave and inputted passwords into her mobile phone. It is one of life's great gifts for a grandchild to be able to 'mother' a grandparent. They will never have that opportunity again.

My mother, with her broken ankle, had been a complicating and complicated presence during my recovery from surgery.

I wanted her, against all reason, to make me well. But even mothers cannot disappear cancer. She was also in pain herself, and frail, her stomach acting up, which made me guilty for not being well enough to look after her. Mothers and daughters and our tangle of love and guilt—it never ends.

What she did do was to tell me to rest, when everyone else was telling me to exercise. She massaged my shoulders gently; she stroked my hair. She took me back for a few seconds to a time when I didn't know what a surgery was, and everything was still ahead, and being brave meant holding back the tears because I came second in the three-legged race that I really, really wanted to win. These were the last days we ever spent together.

The origins of the Jar of Happiness were in the prosaic, *The Complete Guide to Breast Cancer: How to Feel Empowered and Take Control*, the book that I had lying on my bed side. My mother borrowed it to brush up on her Oncolish. But in addition to learning about the Nottingham Prognostic Index and HER2 receptor status, she found a section on tips to get through the early days of a diagnosis. These included a suggestion to start a 'jar of joy'. The idea was for the cancer patient to write notes to herself every time she experienced a micro-joy—birds singing in the morning or a particularly tight hug from a child—and to put these in a jar. These could then be returned to when the patient felt disconsolate—guaranteed to put a smile on even the most chemo-fatigued face. My mother's version of this jar was to write notes to me.

I wake up from a dream that recedes almost immediately, but that leaves behind a feeling of urgency which lingers. It takes several hours before I can identify it. The Jar. The notes. She was saying something to me then, that in the fug of recovery was merely sweet. But I am suddenly certain that there are answers there. I open drawers willy-nilly, slamming them shut and am distraught and in tears, which by now feel like a uniform. It is my older son, who calms me down. He had found the notes and pasted them into a notebook for me to look at during the chemo weeks, but I'd been too ill and distracted to pay them attention. He locates the book. I open it, hands trembling, and every hair on my body stands up.

There are eleven notes. She had not come to me as a colour or a spectre. She knew that an atheist like me needed something more concrete. And so, she had left me her words, written in ink, put in a jar, pasted in a book. She had packed all the essentials I would need in my journey through Grief, like she had when I had left for my first school trip away from home in fifth grade.

4.11.22
I can't begin to count the ways in which I am proud to be your mother.
Muma

5.11.22
When I am with you, it's like 'strawberries, cherries and an angel's kiss in spring.' I love you,
Muma

6.11.22
The date: 27.11.1975
The Place: Willingdon Hospital, N Delhi
The happening: maternity ward abuzz with the news that the most beautiful baby ever had been born, with the largest eyes!
Name: Pallavi!
Muma

7.11.22
Memory
Of a small you coming to my bed, lifting the sheet off my face and saying, 'Are you sleeping Muma....Ok, go to sleep.' Thus shattering all thoughts of sleep. The sweetest!
Muma

8.11.22
You are my pocketful of starlight. Keep shining,
Muma

9.11.22
Have you noticed a sparkle wherever you go?
Muma

10.11.22
Tears are not a measure of bravery, but of your humanity.
Love always,
Muma

11:11:22
Today you told me you get me everything I want. Truth is I got everything I want the day you were born.
Muma

13.11.22
Shine on, like you do, even when storms wait to assail you. They will retreat!
Muma

14.11.22
My heart grows sadder as the time to leave you comes.
Muma

15.11.22
I will miss you Pali but be with you in my thoughts always.
Au Revoir,
Muma

This last bag my mother had packed for me is heavy. But inside it, she'd tucked strawberries, starlight and balm. It is a suitcase I think I will have to carry with me forever. But when I am tired, I can always put it down, open it up and be nourished by what it holds within. I know now that I grieve my mother so, because I loved her so. And that love illuminates the grief into something akin to beauty.

In *Wintering*, Katherine May describes how life's winters can be transformational if you stop resisting the cold and start responding by slowing down. To move the focus away from pushing on with 'normal' life to creating a new one. By snuggling under a blanket and nourishing yourself with books and broth. 'When everything is broken, everything is also up for grabs. That's the gift of winter; its irresistible. Change will happen in its wake, whether we like it or not. We can come out of it wearing a different coat.'

It's been nearly two years since my mother died. Grief takes on new shapes every day. Today it looked like chicken nuggets. She loved them as much as the boys. There has been progress in my journey. I am forging tentative friendships with these shapes, or at least we are now more than mere acquaintances. I am learning to communicate with them, and sometimes we exchange a wry laugh. I wear her earrings, the ones I didn't like.

Bad travellers complain. That's their thing. They don't like the weather, or the food. They long to be in an imagined elsewhere that is better. Where they will be happy. But the good ones find pleasure in the challenges. In learning new ways of communicating and working through initial bafflement to arrive eventually at meaning. They allow their journeys to leave their marks upon them. Because the art of travelling well is never about avoiding cracks, but learning how to let the light in.

EPILOGUE

It is August 2025, and I am back where it began. A year and a half after having typed the first sentence that became this book—'I am eight and prickling with excitement'—I am once again at my husband's family home on Spain's border with Portugal in the remote Sierra de Gata. There is little to do, save travel on the sounds of distant sheep bleating, or allow the mind to drift with the clouds across always-astonishing skies. Astonishing in their vastness, their colour, their clarity. And just as I began, I must now, end. There is a season for everything.

This is a double ending: literary and physical. The book has reached its destination, and after five years in Spain, my family is once again set to take wing. This time we are returning, after sixteen years away, to China. But I know enough of any place, and China more than most, that return is impossible. Just as no man steps into the same river twice—for it is not the same river and he is not the same man—so a very different 'us' will be stepping into a very different Beijing. The future is pregnant with anticipation, but this moment belongs to Spain, my sasural—as the land of a woman's in-laws is called in Hindi. I have lived here for five years, through a pandemic, and cancer and loss, and so much gain.

The decision to move to Madrid had not been an easy one for me. For decades, my Spanish spouse and I had flitted across foreign postings in Asia—China, Japan, Indonesia—places where we shared outsider status. Together, we made silly mistakes while bumbling about learning the syntax of unfamiliar streets. Together, we experienced the humility that comes from not having the right words, and the sense of wonder when you finally chance upon them.

Spain, I believed, would change this equilibrium. I would be the interloper in my husband's home. I feared feeling excluded and stupid, rather than intrepid and curious, as had been our combined wont until then. But there came a moment (in the early months of the pandemic) when moving to Madrid became inevitable, despite my misgivings.

As it transpired, these years have been a masterclass in learning to live well. It is nigh impossible to be sad in this country. Even in the tough months, I only had to step out onto the street to be buoyed by the social energy that crackles from the curbside cafes punctuating the streets like chattering exclamation marks. Inevitably, there were groups of silver-haired ladies enjoying gin and tonics, seated next to young families with toddlers who ran about just on the right side of not-badly-behaved. People smiled and kissed and sometimes shrieked in happiness at bumping unexpectedly into a friend.

A few months ago, on 28 April 2025, most of the Iberian Peninsula suffered a severe electricity outage—trains were stranded, traffic lights malfunctioned, phone and internet coverage faltered, and ATMs stopped working. But the cafés continued to be thronged with de-screened locals making the analogue, human best of it. Pedestrians waved cars on, even as cars tried to give pedestrians the right of way. No one blew their horns. There were no incidents of looting or rioting. I sat on one of Madrid's main avenues without phone connectivity, watching a gaggle of young people practise the Macarena, and felt a deep upswell of love for this city, which has somehow retained a sense of decency in an increasingly indecent world.

And so, I leave you, dear reader, this epilogue as a small diversion from the rest of the book. A sliver of a conventional travelogue (and a listicle to boot):

Ten things to know about Spain

Lunch Is a Brave New World

Lunch in España is what prayer is in Indonesia, haggling in India, and the weather in the UK—the dominant backdrop to life. Ironically, the actual word for lunch in Spanish, *almuerzo*, is among the less useful in the lexicon, because it is invariably replaced by *comida*, which is simply, food. If you say, 'let's meet to eat food,' it is understood that it is lunch that is being talked about.

The Spanish lunch is late, lavish and lingering. On special occasions, like Friday-because-the-weekend-starts-tomorrow, it is epic and epicurean. It can begin at 3 p.m. and last until dinner. The meal often features a three-course *menú del dia* (menu of the day), wine, and *sobremesa*. Literally, 'on the table,' sobremesa refers to the long hours spent sitting around the table after the food has been eaten, shooting the breeze, quaffing coffees that might lead to gin and tonics, because by this time it is often 6 p.m. and so, why not?

Storks on Steeples

The most emblematic motifs associated with Spain include flamenco, tapas and beaches. But for me, it is a stork atop a church steeple, framed by a wide-open sky.

Across the broad belly of the country—Toledo, Extremadura, Castilla-la Mancha the skies are dramatic. The blue is deep, the clouds cotton-candy fluffy and the horizon endless. But every so often a steeple—a church spire, a miraculously intact Roman column, an industrial chimney, an electric pole—comes into view. And perched upon these are gloriously balletic storks, standing like St Simeon, one-legged, upon huge nests of grass and sticks. The birds fly in with muscular grace from Northern Africa every summer to nest. And in their migratory nature, I sense a kindred spirit—one that wishes to soar above borders and make its home in different places that are all equally its own. There is something about the sight of a stork swooping down to rest atop the bell tower of a baroque cathedral that calls out to the soul of every nomad.

Coffee at the Perfect Temperature

Having suffered sugar masquerading as coffee in Indonesia, milk as coffee in India, fancy-pantsy Japanese concoctions and flavoured water in the US, the U2 track 'I still haven't found what I'm looking for' had been the aural backdrop to much of my caffeine-seeking life. Then came the day I sat down in a café in Madrid's Plaza Mayor and ordered a cup. Here, finally, the concept of the milk-coffee-temperature ratio being crucial (and subjective) appeared to have been grasped, for I was served a robust espresso-based starter with the choice of hot (*caliente*) or lukewarm (*templada*) milk in the precise ratio I desired.

And while these days, there is serious man-bun energy in the hipster parts of Madrid—think, charcoal-activated cold brews—there are still enough old-fashioned cafés to be found across Spain, where a *café-con-leche* can be had at the perfect temperature, with a generous pour from the *leche caliente* jug, tempered with a splash of milk from its templada sibling. Bliss.

Dos apellidos is the Norm: Everyone Gets to Have Both Parents' Surnames

In Spain, children take the *apellidos* (surnames) of their fathers *and* mothers. The maternal name only lasts a generation. So, for example, my husband's surname is Arias-Camison Altieri, the 'Altieri' being his mother's family name (or to be precise her father's surname), but our children have the family name Arias-Camison Aiyar. It isn't a perfect solution to gender balance in naming, but better than other patrilineal surname norms.

It does mean Spaniards generally need more space to fill out their appellations on official forms. But it could be worse. They could be South Indian.

The Gypsies Are Indian (or So They Say)

Gitanos or gypsies may be the most iconic demographic of Spain, but it is India that they identify strongly with. I first realised this two decades ago, upon finding myself in a cinch with a gitano flamenco singer in a smoky tavern in Madrid, on a winter night in 2004. I'd been only one amongst the musician's many adoring fans until he learned that I was Indian. 'I am from India too,' he'd said, tapping his chest with an open palm before gathering me up for a hug.

Gitanos, of which there are upwards of 750,000 in Spain, do not have a well-documented history. But they are believed to have entered the region during the fifteenth century. Linguistic analysis of Romani (gypsy) dialects shows that they originated in north-western India and migrated westwards in waves, between 300 BC and AD 600.

At an international Roma summit held in New Delhi in 2016, then Indian External Affairs Minister Sushma Swaraj called the Roma community 'children of India'. 'You are the children of India who migrated and lived in challenging circumstances in foreign lands for centuries. Yet you maintained your Indian identity,' she said.[1]

The Tarde: What Is It?

Philosophers through the ages have pondered philosophical puzzles like 'What is the soul?' But Spain's enduring metaphysical mystery is 'the *tarde*'. The English translation for the word 'afternoon' does little to clarify its ontological status. I have had people wish me '*buenas tarde*' at 9 p.m., a time that does not match the description of 'afternoon' anywhere else.

When someone says they will see you in the 'afternoon,' they most definitely do not mean post-noon as in 12.30 p.m. So, what is the tarde? I posed the question to myriad Spaniards, only to receive myriad responses. A sampling:

> It starts at 2 p.m. and ends at umm…not sure.

It starts at 4 p.m. and ends when the sun sets (which in the summer is after 10 p.m.).
It starts after lunch (which begs the question about lunchtime, another quotidian epoch with insanely fungible boundaries in España).
It starts after 'siesta', which follows lunch (see above).

Suffice to say, eventually the tarde becomes something instinctive. Something you know, when you know. To wield the term with insouciance is to have found your inner Spaniard.

A Catholic Country that Invokes Allah Daily

Given that parts of Spain were under Islamic rule for almost 800 years (from 711 to the fall of Granada in 1492), it is surprising how little overt evidence of this long influence remains. But traces of this history continue to lurk subterraneously in the language. *Ojalá*, which means 'hopefully,' has its root in *insh'allah*. So that every time a Spaniard says anything akin to, 'Hopefully we'll meet soon,' they are etymologically invoking the grace of God (Allah).

Modern Spanish has thousands of words with Arab roots, linking it in a string of lexical pearls to Hindi/Hindustani, given the latter's debt to Persian-mediated Arabic. Consider the words for sugar: *azúcar* in Spanish derives from the Mozarabic (Arabic influenced Spanish that developed between the 7th and 15th centuries) *assúkar*, in turn from the classical Arabic *sukkar*. In Hindustani it is *shakkar*. Or the words for chess: *Ajedrez* in Spanish comes from the Mozarabic *aššaṭran*, which has its root in the classical Arabic, *šiṭranǧ*. In Hindustani, it is *shatranj*.

Breakfast Like Hobbits

In Spain, second breakfast is not something that exists in the pages of a Tolkienist idle, but daily practice. The day begins with a quick first *desayuno* of coffee and maybe a cookie or toast. Enough fuel for about two hours of work, before second breakfast—which is the really fun one.

El *segundo* involves heading to the bar or café down the street (there is zero possibility of a city street without said establishment) with co-workers and scarfing down tostadas, croissants or churros, all washed down with coffee (with milk at your preferred temperature). Second breakfast is an 11 a.m. affair. Its necessity becomes evident when one realises that lunch is a temporally amorphous event that may occur deep into the mysterious tarde.

The 'Chino' Is an Institution

If Japan has the *konbini* (convenience store), and the UK, the corner shop, Spain's equivalent is the '*chino*'. This nickname for *alimentaciónes*—daily life's answer to everything from stationery to snacks and toilet paper—derives from the fact that most of these shops are run by Chinese immigrants. I've even heard a corner shop referred to as a '*chino español*' because it was operated by a Spaniard.

'Chinos' speak of two aspects of Spanish culture that are noteworthy. First, the deep cultural linkages that the Chinese immigrant community has formed here in the space of two decades. Between 1998 and 2019, the Chinese population of Spain increased sixteen-fold.[2]

Second, Spain may be grouped geographically and economically in the "West," but it remains a stranger to the political correctness that is the contemporary hallmark of most countries thus designated.

Kiss-Kiss

To live in Spain is to kiss and be kissed (twice, on each cheek): by new acquaintances and old friends, aunties and children, and some very random people. Among the more unlikely kissers I know is my dentist, who always kisses me goodbye moments after she has been staring into the netherworld of my mouth.

Spain takes you in and makes you part of the family. It's not just in the kisses but also in the affectionate way people address each other, as *cariño* (dear) and *guapa* (beautiful). I even got called *reina* (queen) by an Amazon delivery guy once!

Hoyos,
Sierra de Gata,
August 2025

ACKNOWLEDGEMENTS

Profoundest thanks to my family: Julio, Ishaan, Nico, Shekhar, Swaminathan, Gang.

Shukriya to the whole Global Jigsaw family—all the followers, readers and well-wishers of my newsletter, which birthed several of the ideas that made it to this book.

Much gratitude to stormy weather friends for phone calls, hospital-ferrying, care packages, books, soaps, visits, walks, jigsaw puzzles, cake, and jobs: Katia Harling, Alejandra Kindelan, Ana Maria Vidaurre, Priya Christian, Mary Ganguli, Preeti Kothari, Sulay Sinha, Eva Borreguero, Christine Roberts, Suranya Aiyar, Yamini Aiyar, Tarana Sawhney, Sukhdev Sandhu, Ritika Jhanji, Shweta Rathore, Maya Mathew, Tuva Kahrs, Shiraz Sidhva, Moko sensei, Shelley Sacks, Yumiko Watanabe, Yoko Renner, Wakako Chen, Carla Sezmo, and Iona Oliviera.

Muchisimas gracias for the agenting, publishing and marketing heroes behind this book: Ranjana Sengupta at A Suitable Agency, and Karthika and Amrita at Westland. Also, to Vedika for a sterling job with the copyediting.

I owe my health to Dras Calvo and Ortega.

Thanks for many of the reporting opportunities, the recountings of which have made it to this book to: N Ram, Siddharth Varadarajan, Sanjaya Baru, T.N. Ninan, Mukund Padmanabhan, Gwen Robinson.

Gratitude for favours, opportunities and epiphanies to an assortment of angels who have made my travels better, including

Jean-Pierre Lehmann, Jeff Wasserstrom, Mahesh Rangarajan, Gonzalo Garland, Javier Moro and Amruta Patil.

And finally, and always, it is to my mother, Gitanjali, that thanks are owed, for this book, for this life, for all the journeys.

NOTES

Beginning

1. Michel de Montaigne, *On the Education of Children*, trans. Charles Cotton (Doubleday, 1947 [c.1580]), p. 40.

Chapter 1. Books

1. Katherine Rundell, *Why You Should Read Children's Books, Even Though You Are So Old and Wise* (Bloomsbury, London, 2019).
2. G. K. Chesterton, *What I Saw in America* (Dodd, Mead and Company, New York, 1922).
3. Full quote: 'The only traveller with real soul I've ever met was an office boy who worked in a company where I was at one time employed. This young lad collected brochures on different cities, countries and travel companies; he had maps, some torn out of newspapers, others begged from one place or another; he cut out pictures of landscapes, engravings of exotic costumes, paintings of boats and ships from various journals and magazines. He would visit travel agencies on behalf of some real or hypothetical company, possibly the actual one in which he worked, and ask for brochures on Italy or India, brochures giving details of sailings between Portugal and Australia. He knew exactly which trains one had to catch to go from Paris to Bucharest; which trains one took to cross England; and in his garbled pronunciation of the strange names hung the bright certainty of the greatness of his soul. Now he probably lives like a dead man, but perhaps one day, when he's old, he'll remember that to dream of Bordeaux is not only better, but truer, than actually to arrive in Bordeaux.'

4. *Other Routes: 1500 Years of African and Asian Travel Writing*, ed. Tabish Khair (Signal Books Ltd, Oxford, 2006).

Chapter 2. Illness

1. National Cancer Institute, *Reproductive History and Cancer Risk*, https://www.cancer.gov/about-cancer/causes-prevention/risk/hormones/reproductive-history-fact-sheet.
2. I. Brosens, "Oral Contraceptives, Nuns, and Cancer," The Lancet 380, no. 9852 (2012): 1014–15, https://doi.org/10.1016/S0140-6736(12)61014-9.
3. Fiona Conway-Jones, "Our Milestones: A Radical Change That Improved Breast Cancer Surgery," Cancer Research UK, October 2, 2017, https://news.cancerresearchuk.org/2017/10/02/our-milestones-a-radical-change-that-improved-breast-cancer-surgery/.
4. Siddhartha Mukherjee, *The Emperor of All Maladies: A Biography of Cancer* (Scribner, New York, 2010).
5. Ibid. The word for cancer first appeared around 400 BC from the Greek word for crab, karkinos. The tumor enveloped in a net of swollen blood vessels reminded Hippocrates of a crab in the sand with its legs spread out in a circle.
6. Jessica J. Hsu et al., "Perceived versus Patient-Reported Significance of Surgeon Gender in Breast Reconstruction," *Plastic and Reconstructive Surgery* 148, no. 4 (October 1, 2021): 720–728, https://doi.org/10.1097/PRS.0000000000008311.
7. American Cancer Society, "How Chemotherapy Drugs Work," https://www.cancer.org/cancer/managing-cancer/treatment-types/chemotherapy/how-chemotherapy-drugs-work.html.
8. European Commission, Joint Research Centre, Breast Cancer Burden in the EU, https://ecis.jrc.ec.europa.eu/pdf/Breast_cancer_factsheet-Oct_2020.pdf.

Chapter 3. Language

1. Mao pushed for Putonghua, a newly standardised idiom based on the language spoken in the nation's capital, Beijing, to become what we now refer to as 'Chinese.' This took considerable social

engineering to achieve. Prior to the 1950s, Han Chinese spoke nine main tongues that were, in large part, mutually unintelligible when spoken. These included Mandarin, which became the basis for Putonghua, Wu (of which Shanghainese is part), Xiang, Gan, Jin, Kejia, Yue, Northern Min and Southern Min each with many sub dialects. In order to consolidate state power, facilitate communication between the Chinese peoples and to promote literacy, Mao Zedong 'reformed' Chinese to make Putonghua (literally- the common speech) the national standard.

2. 6.8 per cent say it is their second. Forty-three other idioms have more first language speakers than English. Those who speak just 'some' English account for ten per cent of citizens. In contrast, Hindi is spoken as a first language by 528 million people, or almost forty-four per cent of all Indians. Census 2011.
3. Jing Tsu, *Kingdom of Characters: A Tale of Language, Obsession, and Genius in Modern China* (London: Allen Lane, 2022).
4. Sullivan, Michael. *The Three Perfections: Chinese Painting, Poetry, and Calligraphy*. Rev. ed. New York: George Braziller, 1999.
5. Michael Sullivan, *The Three Perfections: Chinese Painting, Poetry, and Calligraphy*, rev. ed. (New York: George Braziller, 1999).
6. The date is contested by the Dutch … 1948.

Chapter 5. Passportism

1. Jasmine Garsd, "The Reaction as Trump's Travel Ban on Citizens from a Dozen Countries Takes Effect," *NPR*, June 9, 2025, https://www.npr.org/2025/06/09/nx-s1-5427998/trump-travel-ban-countries-immigration-enforcement.
2. Shahnaz Habibi, *Airplane Mode: An Irreverent History of Travel* (New York: Catapult, 2023).
3. "Global Passport Power Rank 2025," PassportIndex, https://www.passportindex.org/byRank.php.
4. Martin Lloyd, *The Passport: The History of Man's Most Travelled Document* (Stroud: Sutton Publishing, 2003).

   John C. Torpey, *The Invention of the Passport: Surveillance, Citizenship and the State*, Cambridge Studies in Law and Society (Cambridge: Cambridge University Press, 2018), i.

5. Kam Wing Chan, *Urbanization with Chinese Characteristics: The Hukou System and Migration* (London: Routledge, 2019).
6. Giulia Pines, "The Contentious History of the Passport," *National Geographic*, May 16, 2017, HYPERLINK "https://www.nationalgeographic.com/history/article/a-history-of-the-passport?utm_source=chatgpt.com"https://www.nationalgeographic.com/history/article/a-history-of-the-passport.
7. Tabish Khair, "The Colour of Our Passports," *The Hindu*, December 21, 2003.
8. Ueli Gyr, *The History of Tourism: Structures on the Path to Modernity*, trans. [if applicable] (2010), https://www.ieg-ego.eu/en/threads/europe-on-the-road/the-history-of-tourism.
9. Tabish Khair, 2003, The Hindu, The Colour of our Passports.

Chapter 6. Reporting

1. Lucy Hornby, "On the Outside Looking In: China Expels American Journalists," *Nieman Reports*, March 20, 2020, https://niemanreports.org/articles/china-expels-american-journalists/.
2. Sandhya Krishnan and Neeraj Hatekar, "Understanding the Burgeoning Indian Middle Class through its Expenditure and Asset-Ownership Patterns," in *The Middle Class in World Society: Negotiations, Diversities and Lived Experiences*, ed. C. Suter, S. Madheswaran, and B.P. Vani (London: Routledge, 2020), 219–41, https://www.taylorfrancis.com/chapters/edit/10.4324/9781003049630-13/understanding-burgeoning-indian-middle-class-expenditure-asset-ownership-patterns-sandhya-krishnan-neeraj-hatekar.
3. In her 2002 book, *Whole Numbers and Half Truths*, Rukmini S calculates that only three per cent of Indians own five basic consumer goods (a motor vehicle; a television; a refrigerator; cooler/air conditioner; and a computer).
4. Association for Democratic Reforms (ADR), "139 BJP Leaders, 49 Congress Members on List of 306 MPs Facing Criminal Charges," ADR India, December 9, 2023, https://adrindia.org/content/139-bjp-leaders-49-congress-members-list-306-mps-facing-criminal-charges-adr-report.

5. Author(s), "Title of Article," *The Washington Post*, October 19, 2008, https://www.washingtonpost.com/wp-dyn/content/article/2008/10/19/AR2008101900658.html?hpid=sec-world.
6. Steven Erlanger, "When a Border Shapes More Than Territory," *The New York Times*, March 4, 2012, https://www.nytimes.com/2012/03/04/world/europe/when-a-border-shapes-more-than-territory.html.
7. Pallavi Aiyar, "The Pakistanisation of Indonesia," *The Hindu*, June 17, 2013, https://www.thehindu.com/opinion/op-ed/the-pakistanisation-of-indonesia/article4815062.ece.
8. Pallavi Aiyar and Chin Hwee Tan, "India and Indonesia: Twins Under the Skin," *Milken Institute Review*, July 27, 2015, https://www.milkenreview.org/articles/india-and-indonesia-twins-under-the-skin.
9. Jamie Oliver's paella recipe is panned online, *BBC News*, October 4, 2016, https://www.bbc.com/news/world-europe-37555389.

Epilogue

1. IANS, "Call to Recognise Romas as Indian Diaspora," *Business Standard*, February 14, 2016, https://www.business-standard.com/article/news-ians/call-to-recognise-romas-as-indian-diaspora-116021400771_1.html.
2. "Así ha crecido la comunidad china en Espaşa desde 1998," EPData, https://www.epdata.es/asi-crecido-comunidad-china-espana-1998/8b563ccc-e003-42e9-95fb-72430a74d102.